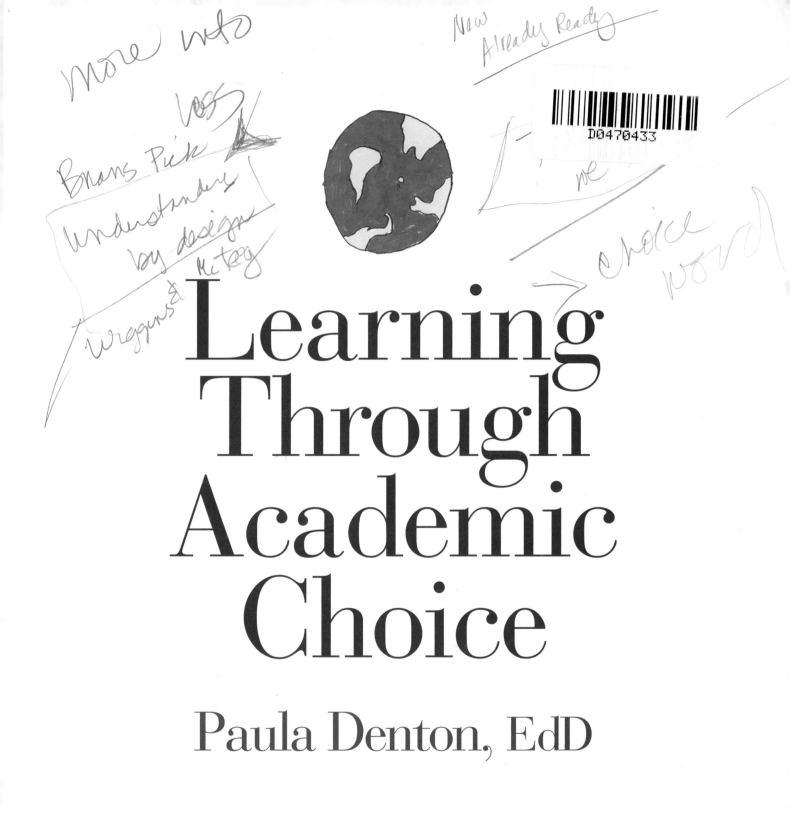

Learning Through Academic Choice

Paula Denton, EdD

STRATEGIES FOR TEACHERS SERIES

In this book, there are many stories based on real classroom events. However, in order to respect the privacy of students, names and many identifying characteristics of students and situations have been changed.

ISBN-13: 978-1-892989-14-7
ISBN-10: 1-892989-14-X

Library of Congress control number 2005921483

Photographs: Paula Denton, Peter Wrenn

Cover and book design: Woodward Design

NORTHEAST FOUNDATION FOR CHILDREN, INC.
85 Avenue A, Suite 204
P. O. Box 718
Turners Falls, MA 01376-0718
800-360-6332

www.responsiveclassroom.org

09 08 07 06   6 5 4 3 2

We would like to thank the Shinnyo-en Foundation for its generous support of the development of this book.

The mission of the Shinnyo-en Foundation is "to bring forth deeper compassion among humankind, to promote greater harmony, and to nurture future generations toward building more caring communities."

16th

ACKNOWLEDGMENTS

This book builds upon the work of many educators who have shared their approaches to Academic Choice over the years, beginning with faculty at Antioch New England Graduate School—*Jane Miller, David Sobel,* and *Heidi Watts*—who first alerted me to the value of choice within curricula. My colleagues at the Greenfield Center School were also essential to the development of this approach to teaching especially those with whom I worked most closely: *Chip Wood, Ruth Charney, Marlynn Clayton, Jay Lord,* and *Roxann Kriete.*

Colleagues affiliated with Northeast Foundation for Children (NEFC) who have contributed ideas, shared experiences, and helped enormously in the development of this book include *Adam Berkin, Marcia Bradley, Melissa Correa-Connolly, Linda Crawford, Caltha Crowe, Carol Davis, Sadie Fischesser, Pamela Porter,* and *Michele Sabia.*

Mary Beth Forton, associate director at NEFC, has been a great cheerleader and guide to the entire process of writing the book from initial inspiration to shaping the content and obtaining feedback from readers. She responded to my questions and worries with speedy and reassuring responses.

Lynn Bechtel, a most careful reader and listener, was the editor and project manager. She has taken my words and crafted them into a clear and cohesive book.

Laura Simmons provided a careful and thoughtful copyediting and proofreading.

Leslie and Jeff Woodward designed the book, as they always do, with an eye for detail and a deep concern for its aesthetic qualities.

Teachers *Sharon Ralls, Sue Majka, Marty Kennedy, Margaret Berry, Pam Thompson, Lara Webb, Wendy Tang,* and *Babs Freeman-Loftis* kindly allowed us to take photographs in their classrooms.

I have also observed and discussed Academic Choice with teachers and children in many classrooms around the country and I have learned from all of them. They each influenced the ideas in this book. Some of the most prominent among these teachers include *Patty Lawrence, Lisa Pion, Ken Kowalski, Margaret Berry, Cindy Leonard, Dana Januszka, Sharon Ralls, Marty Kennedy, Donna Petit, Kay Mc Hugh, Debra Armento, Babs Freeman-Loftis, Leah Carson, Mark Emmons, Andy Dousis, Mike Anderson, Sally McCarthy, Karen Baum, Kristin Kugelman,* and *Ellen Schwartz.*

Sue Majka deserves a special mention for her major investment of time and energy into developing Academic Choice in her classroom and for sharing the ups and downs of her process with me over the course of an entire year. I learned a great deal from her experiences and reflections.

For those dedicated teachers who continually seek ways to make learning joyful and meaningful for each of their students.

TABLE OF CONTENTS

Introduction

A strategy for structuring many kinds of lessons and activities, Academic Choice is a powerful tool for increasing students' motivation and academic skills as well as for building community in the classroom. Over the past twenty years, I have observed hundreds of Academic Choice lessons in classrooms around the country. Some of these Academic Choice lessons were simple and brief (e.g., choose one of three teacher-defined ways to practice your spelling words); others were more complex and extended over several days (e.g., choose an insect to study, learn ten facts about it, and choose how to show what you've learned to the rest of the class). But time after time, in both simple lessons and complex, I've seen students working independently, with excitement and curiosity, eager to learn and to share their learning with others.

Here are a couple of quick glimpses of Academic Choice in action:

A first grade class studies oil slicks

First grade teacher Lisa Pion used Academic Choice to structure a study of oil slicks. Children had dipped feathers, fur, and tiles (to simulate a turtle's shell) in cups of cooking oil to find out how greasy the animals would get in an oil slick. Lisa then posed a challenge: How can you get the oil off the "animals"? The children could choose ways to solve this problem. "Some tried to wash the feathers and things with soap; some tried to wipe it off with napkins. Some even tried to blow or suck it off with straws!" Lisa said.

After the children completed these experiments, Lisa offered them several ways that they could report on their results to the group. The children chose from a list that included telling about what they did, writing a narrative, drawing, creating plays, writing songs, making up games, and writing poems.

Throughout the afternoon, the children stayed focused and did high-quality work. And they helped each other. "A couple of children who have a hard time with reading and writing asked other kids 'Will you help me write?' They were so invested in their work that they chose to take risks to do things that were hard for them," Lisa said.

A fourth grade class finishes a unit on rocks and minerals

Introduction

At the end of a unit on rocks and minerals, fourth grade teacher Sue Majka asked students to choose six major concepts they had learned and then choose among several different ways of demonstrating their understanding of these concepts. Students were excited about the possibilities. In fact, they were so engaged in the project that many of them asked if it was OK to show concepts that they had learned outside of school. "I was thrilled!" Sue said. "They'd been going home at night and finding out more information about rocks and minerals simply because they were interested, not because I made an assignment."

The positive impact of providing choices

These two teachers, like many teachers I've talked with, recognize the value of offering choices to students. To help understand why choice provision has such a positive impact on learning, I turned to research. I found thirty-two studies that looked at the outcome of choice provision in grades K–12 (see Appendix E for more detailed information about these studies). Most of this research demonstrated that when students have choices in their learning, they become highly engaged and productive. They are excited about learning and sharing their knowledge. They are likely to think more deeply and creatively, work with more persistence, and willingly use a range of academic skills and strategies. In addition, educational researchers—and many teachers—report that students get along better with each other, resolve conflicts more independently, and actually reduce the number of problem behaviors in the classroom when they have regular opportunities to make choices in their learning.

Academic Choice in the *Responsive Classroom®* approach

Teachers have always incorporated many kinds of choices into daily lessons: Choose six of the following ten questions to answer. Choose a mammal to study in depth. Choose a partner to work with or a place to work. Decide whether to work on an assignment during quiet time at school or later at home.

These are all valuable choices but they are not Academic Choice as we define it. Choices about whether to work alone or with a partner, where to work, and when to work can enhance learning and help children practice making good choices, but they are not Academic Choice.

Academic Choice in the *Responsive Classroom* approach is limited to two kinds of choices that students can make—what to learn (content) and/or how to learn (process). In addition, every Academic Choice lesson always has three phases: planning, working, and reflecting. During planning, children decide what they are going to do and sometimes plan how they'll do it. During the working phase, they complete their chosen task. And during the reflecting phase, they reflect on the work they've done and the learning that has occurred.

Why is Academic Choice so powerful?

When teachers use Academic Choice to structure lessons, children become purposeful, competent learners who connect to each other in positive ways. Thinking back to her first experiences with Academic Choice, Sue Majka said, "I loved looking out and seeing all these clusters of kids so busy and focused on their work, so happy with what they were doing."

Reasons why Academic Choice has these results include:

- Academic Choice supports children's intrinsic motivation to learn.

- Academic Choice gives students opportunities to see each other's good ideas and learn from each other.

- Academic Choice addresses a range of skill levels, strengths, and interests.

- The three phases of Academic Choice maximize children's learning.

Academic Choice supports children's intrinsic motivation to learn

Students in Sue Majka's fourth grade class were studying long division. To help them practice, Sue gave them choices of different kinds of games to create. One student got really engaged in making a board game, similar to Chutes and Ladders. "But he had never learned how to divide," Sue says, "and it had lots of division problems on it that players needed to solve in order to move ahead. When I asked him how he would know if someone got the right answer to a

Introduction

problem, he realized he needed to learn how to divide. He was able to focus and learn how to divide in one day!"

Sue and the long-division wary student learned firsthand about a positive impact of Academic Choice. When children have choices about how and/or what they learn, their intrinsic desire to learn increases.

To understand this, I turned to self-determination theory. According to self-determination theory, we all have an innate need to feel competent, to belong, and to have some degree of freedom or autonomy, and meeting these needs motivates much of our behavior. When these needs are met, we are free to pursue constructive learning experiences. By contrast, when we feel that we don't have any control or input into our experiences and environments, when we feel incompetent or isolated, we tend to become disengaged, cynical, and alienated. An overemphasis on external direction and on motivators such as rewards and punishments can encourage these negative feelings. (Deci and Ryan 1985)

In the example above, Academic Choice allowed the reluctant student to meet his innate need for competence, freedom, and belonging. Because he could choose how to practice the math skill, he had a sense of control over his learning. His desire to create a useful game motivated him to learn a difficult skill. And designing a game that other students could enjoy promoted a sense of belonging and allowed other students to value his contributions.

Academic Choice gives students opportunities to appreciate each other's good ideas and learn from each other

Joe, a student who has difficulty with reading, makes an insightful comment about a story that the teacher read to the class.

Marika's approach to learning the multiplication tables inspires other students to try a new strategy.

Shy Enrique delights his classmates with the song he wrote to depict the main character in the novel Bud, Not Buddy.

Academic Choice gives children many opportunities to learn from one another, whether it's a new fact about electricity or a new strategy for solving a math problem. For example, during the working phase, students might consult

with each other informally about their work, and during the reflecting phase, children often have an opportunity to display their work and talk about how they achieved their final result.

Academic Choice also provides ways for children to discover shared interests. In the process, they become more collaborative and develop friendly relationships with more classmates. And, although Academic Choice is not a magic bullet, it can help children whose behavior sometimes creates problems to become more cooperative and invested in school.

First grade teacher Lisa Pion sums up the positive impact of Academic Choice on social learning when she says, "During Academic Choice, the kids get to see each other in whole new ways. They discover each other's hidden talents and gain new respect for each other."

Introduction

Academic Choice addresses a range of skill levels, strengths, and interests

During science period in a first grade classroom, students had been examining the differences between objects that float and objects that sink. To demonstrate what they had learned, they chose from a list of six options:

- Create a Venn diagram or pictograph.

- Give a written or oral summary.

- Make a picture book or comic strip.

- Write a song.

- Create a model.

- Perform an experiment.

Each of these choices draws on different strengths and abilities. When students can work from their areas of strength and personal interest, they are more likely to feel invested in their work and to draw personal meaning from it than when they are doing teacher assigned work. Teachers recognize this benefit of providing choices. A study I did in 2003 (Denton 2003) showed that many teachers value Academic Choice because it allows them to differentiate instruction to meet a wider range of their students' needs.

In addition, educational thinkers are coming to believe that multiple intelligences and learning styles are dynamic rather than static traits. (Gutierrez and Rogoff 2003; Klein 2003) The approach that works best for any individual will change depending on the content and the context of the learning. Recent research also indicates that people might use several learning styles in a given task. (Klein 2003) Academic Choice allows teachers to observe students' preferred learning styles and interests over time and to tailor lessons to fit shifts in interests and aptitudes and continue meeting a wide range of learning styles and needs.

The three phases of Academic Choice
(planning, working, reflecting) maximize children's learning

Much of the power of Academic Choice resides in this cycle of planning, working, and reflecting, which reflects a natural cycle of learning. Early twentieth century theorists Jean Piaget (Piaget 1923/1959) and John Dewey (Dewey 1938/1963) said that in order to learn most effectively, children must initiate activities based on self-generated goals, actively interact with concrete materials, explore, try out ideas, solve problems, and then make sense of their experiences through reflective thought. As children engage in this cycle of learning, their knowledge base gradually becomes broader and more sophisticated.

Lately, research on the human brain has added more evidence that the planning, working, and reflecting cycle provides an optimal sequence for learning. According to brain researchers, we learn most when we attach a sense of personal relevance to a learning task. To do this, we need to have "compelling goals" (Jensen 1998, 67), active interactions that allow for mistakes and self-corrections, and regular opportunities to disengage from activity and reflect upon what we have done.

To see how these theories apply to Academic Choice, let's take a look at a simple Academic Choice lesson designed to help children practice math computation skills (lesson inspired by first grade teacher Leah Carson). In a first grade class, the teacher wants children to practice subtracting from ten. She gives students a list of ten problems.

- **Planning:** They can choose which eight of the ten problems to solve, and they can choose one activity from a list of five to help them solve the problems. Although the teacher defines the overall goal, students can initiate a specific path to that goal based on their own sense of what's the right level of challenge.

- **Working:** The five options include an activity called Under the Cup in which students use plastic bears as counters; a game called Spinners in which students spin a dial twice and subtract the smaller number spun from the larger number spun; a computer game called Number Maze; an activity called Stickers in which students solve the problems, then use stickers to illustrate the problem and the answer; and an activity called Bead Bars in which students use bead bars to calculate differences. In each choice, students need to figure out a strategy, test out the strategy, and then make adjustments based on the results.

- **Reflecting:** At the end of the working period, students will get a chance to think back on what they did and answer a focusing question such as "How did you solve the problems and why did you choose this approach?" This allows them to make sense out of their concrete experiences.

At the end of the lesson, children will not only have gained practice in subtracting, they will also have learned thinking skills and strategies that will help them get the most out of their learning.

Learning to use Academic Choice

At this point, I can imagine teachers saying, "Academic Choice is an intriguing strategy but how can I find time to learn about it and implement it?" In this book, I guide teachers step-by-step through the process of introducing Academic Choice into their teaching. In Part One, teachers will learn about the steps they can take to build a strong foundation for Academic Choice. In Part Two, teachers will follow a teacher through each phase of an Academic Choice lesson. And in Part Three, teachers will learn the details of planning Academic Choice lessons. Throughout the book, I include examples of Academic Choice in action as well as specific lesson plan ideas and examples of both teacher and student planning and assessment formats.

I encourage you to start slowly. Read a section of the book, try out a new idea or two, then read some more. Gradually, build to the point where you offer one or two Academic Choice lessons a week. Soon you and the students will experience firsthand the many benefits of Academic Choice—and you might find you incorporate this strategy on a daily basis.

Works Cited

Deci, Edward L. and Richard M. Ryan. 1985. *Intrinsic Motivation and Self-Determination in Human Behavior.* New York: Plenum Press.

Denton, Paula. 2003. *Teachers' Understanding of the Rationale for Providing Academic Choices to Students and Their Perceptions of Obstacles to Its Implementation.* Unpublished manuscript. University of Massachusetts at Amherst.

Dewey, John. 1938/1963. *Experience and Education.* New York: Collier MacMillan Publishing.

Gutierrez, Kris D. and Barbara Rogoff. 2003. "Cultural Ways of Learning: Individual Traits or Repertoires of Practice." *Educational Researcher* 32(5): 19-25.

Jensen, Eric. 1998. *Teaching with the Brain in Mind.* Alexandria, VA: Association for Supervision and Curriculum Development (ASCD).

Klein, Perry D. 2003. "Rethinking the Multiplicity of Cognitive Resources and Curricular Representations: Alternatives to 'Learning Styles' and 'Multiple Intelligences.'" *Journal of Curriculum Studies* 35(1): 45-81.

Piaget, Jean. 1923/1959. *The Language and Thought of the Child.* New York: The Humanities Press, Inc.

PART ONE

BUILDING A STRONG FOUNDATION FOR ACADEMIC CHOICE

Before implementing Academic Choice, it is important to prepare the children for success. Children need to have experience with working independently, making choices, and regulating their own behavior. They need to understand how to use basic materials and have a repertoire of academic skills to draw on. And they need to treat each other kindly and work collaboratively. Without this strong foundation, attempts at Academic Choice might be problematic, as the following example illustrates.

A good idea that didn't quite work

Second grade teacher Mr. McManus has just learned about Academic Choice and thinks it is a great way to structure a readers' workshop.

He gathers the students on the meeting rug next to the whiteboard. "Okay, gang, we're going to do things differently today. While I work with reading groups, the rest of you will work on one of these activities based on the book you chose to read for independent reading. Each of the choices is a way for you to help us get to know the book." He points to the whiteboard where he has listed:

a. Act out a scene from the book.

b. Write a different ending for the story.

c. Draw a character from the book.

"You may choose which of these three things you'd like to do, and I'll write your name under that choice." He briefly explains each choice. "Any questions?" he asks.

The children look at each other with grins and sit up straighter.

"Can we act out any scene from our book?" asks one boy.

"Yes, you get to decide," says Mr. McManus.

"Sondra and I read the same book. Can we write the story ending together?" asks Amy, who sits with her arm thrown around Sondra's shoulder.

"Well, sure, as long as you work quietly. This is your choice! Okay, who wants to act out a scene?"

The children quickly make their choices. While Mr. McManus begins to settle in with his reading group, the rest of the class happily begins to prepare their skits, write their story endings, or draw.

Amy pulls a chair next to Sondra at her desk, and the two of them begin to discuss ideas for a story ending. "Millie turns into a princess," Sondra proposes.

"Okay, and she has a white horse named Archie," Amy adds.

"A horse! No! I want her to have a kitten," says Sondra.

Building A Strong Foundation

"Why do you always have to have kittens? I want a horse for a change!" Amy pouts. The two girls continue to argue, their voices becoming louder and louder.

Meanwhile, Rico and Sean flip through a copy of the book they have both read, looking for a scene to act out. "I like what happens right at the beginning," says Sean. "There's lots of action."

Rico tries to pull the book away from him. "Let me see. I wanna see what else we can do."

"No, this is the best scene to do." Their voices rise as they argue about where to begin. Mr. McManus gives them a warning frown.

The noise level rises as several children enter the class library and start talking to Rico and Sean about who will be on kickball teams at recess.

"It's too noisy in here! Please keep your voices quiet," Mr. McManus calls from his seat with the reading group.

A moment later, Katrina stands at his shoulder. "I need a purple marker for my drawing," she says, "and I can't find one."

"I'll help you find more markers in a minute," he replies while Ina continues to read aloud. Katrina trots away and begins to search the cabinets for more markers.

As Mr. McManus tries to give his full attention to the reading group, the rest of the class wanders, argues, daydreams, gossips, and searches for books, ideas, and supplies. A few do spend some time planning skits or drawing. The writers write nothing.

At the end of the session, no one has accomplished much, and many of the children are cranky and restless. Mr. McManus is relieved when the period is over and decides not to hold a representing meeting because students have done so little work. "So much for Academic Choice!" he thinks. "Back to assigned worksheets tomorrow."

What went wrong?

Mr. McManus planned an Academic Choice session that began with excited students and great potential, but ended with less than exciting results. It had seemed simple enough when he planned it. He offered three choices that he was pretty sure the children could do. They had all dramatized scenes from books before, many loved to write stories, and they must have all drawn characters from books at some time during their schooling. He also divided the session into times for student planning, working, and reflecting as recommended. Why didn't it work?

In fact, the children responded to this particular Academic Choice session in very predictable ways. Although Mr. McManus had carefully planned this particular lesson, he had not spent time teaching students the skills they would need to complete effective Academic Choice projects. Without a clear sense of how to make good choices, work independently, and collaborate productively, they floundered.

Part One

Building a strong foundation

"Part One: Building a Strong Foundation for Academic Choice" consists of two chapters. In Chapter One, "Teaching the Skills Needed for Success with Academic Choice," you will learn about teaching the social and work skills needed for effective Academic Choice. Specifically, you will learn how to teach students to:

1. Make and reflect on choices

2. Work independently

3. Do a variety of academic activities

4. Work collaboratively

In Chapter Two, "Guided Discovery," you'll learn about teaching children to use materials carefully and creatively through a process called Guided Discovery.

Chapter One

TEACHING THE SKILLS NEEDED FOR SUCCESS WITH ACADEMIC CHOICE

At first glance, implementing Academic Choice might seem like a fairly easy process. Plan the lesson, offer the choices, then watch as the children happily complete their chosen work. But as Mr. McManus's experience illustrates, there's preparation required for successful implementation of Academic Choice.

Teach students how to make and reflect on choices

A crucial element in ensuring successful Academic Choice lessons is teaching children how to make wise choices. To make good choices, children need to have experience with making decisions for themselves, acting on their own initiative, and reflecting on the outcomes of their decisions. But students come to us with a range of backgrounds and skills, and many have little experience with independent decision making. They may be overwhelmed when given choices and refuse to decide on anything, or they may make decisions based upon impulse or random selection rather than reasoning and self-knowledge.

Some children will choose an activity because they think it will be easy to complete and in the process choose something that isn't very interesting or challenging. Others will choose an activity because children they admire have chosen it, not because they feel a personal attraction to the activity itself. As a result, students may not be able to settle down and focus on their work. They may become overly frustrated because they chose tasks that do not match their current interests; they may become sloppy with tasks they chose for their ease and speed of completion. In the process, they lose the benefits of Academic Choice.

To help children experience the positive impact of making choices, teachers need to start small. I often begin by asking children to make decisions as a group, then I move to simple individual choices. I save paired decision making until everyone is ready to work on collaborative work skills.

Teaching Students How to Make Good Choices

1. Offer the whole group a simple either-or choice

2. Model a strategy for making individual choices

Teaching the Skills Needed for Success

Offer the whole group a simple either-or choice

Making choices as a group is a big focus during the first weeks of school, but I also find that children benefit from occasional practice with making choices throughout the year. When children participate in whole group planning, those who have the most difficulty with making choices can learn from the thoughts and actions of more savvy classmates.

In the first weeks of school, I offer the group a simple, straightforward choice. For example, I might ask children whether they would prefer to line up in alphabetical order or in a boy-girl pattern for the day. I ask some volunteers to state their preference and reasons for it, and then call for a vote (with heads down and eyes covered to encourage independent thinking).

At the end of the day or the session in which they put their choice into action, I take five minutes and ask them to reflect on how their choice worked for the group. At this point, I ask open-ended questions (see Chapter Two for more information about open-ended questions) to encourage reflective thought. In the example above, if children chose to line up in a boy-girl pattern, I might ask, "How did lining up in a boy-girl pattern work for the group?"

I often ask the children to share their thoughts with a partner first, so all have a chance to talk. This also helps students formulate their thoughts and opinions before attempting to speak before the entire group. Next, I ask a few volunteers to share their thoughts with the class. I might end by asking all the students to show thumbs up or thumbs down to indicate how well they thought the choice worked.

The following day students might choose between two new patterns for lining up and follow the same procedures for planning and reflecting. Alternatively, I might pose a different type of choice for the group. There are many possibilities and the ideas will vary according to each class and teacher's situation. The following list provides a starting point:

- Seating arrangements (desks arranged in groups of four or groups of six, for example)

- Which of two read-aloud books the teacher will read

- Which of two or three ways to form small groups (by birthdays, clothing colors, or number of siblings, for example)

- Which greeting or activity to do in Morning Meeting or circle time

- Which of two homework assignments to do at school and which to do at home

- How much time to allot for cleanup at the end of a day or a lesson (three minutes, five minutes, or seven minutes, for example)

Chapter One

Model a strategy for making individual choices

I also help children learn to make good choices by offering them simple, fail-proof choices to make individually. For example, students might choose one of two math worksheets to complete. Since both worksheets meet my goal of practicing computation, students can't make a bad choice. Although some children will think carefully about this decision, not all children have the skills for reflective

decision making. So, when I first offer such choices, I use a think-aloud strategy to model the decision-making process for the whole class.

"Hmmm, which one should I pick?" I might say with a wrinkled brow. "These two worksheets are a little different. With one, you have to do twenty problems and when you get the answers, they give you clues so that you can decode the secret message. That's kind of fun. With this other worksheet, you only do eighteen problems and the answers tell you what color to put in each shape so that it makes a picture. The first sheet has more problems, but I really like secret codes. I think I'll do the first sheet." I might also ask one or two of the children to volunteer a reason that someone might choose to do the worksheet that involves coloring.

Teaching the Skills Needed for Success

When I present the options another day, I might simply ask a few students for their thoughts about the advantages of each option. At the end of the session, children reflect on whether they are satisfied with the decision they made and why they feel that way. This gives them experience in critical thinking; over time more and more students will be able to think independently and critically about the choices they make.

Here are some more ideas for simple choices that students can make as individuals:

- Which one of two mathematics problems will you solve? (Later, the choice could be more complex—which five of eight mathematics problems will you solve?)

- Choose a pencil, pen, or marker to copy your spelling words.

- Work at an assigned desk, on the meeting rug, or at the group table in the classroom.

- Choose among three characters in a story about which to answer questions.

- Choose whether to practice vocabulary words by copying them along with definitions or by completing a ready-made worksheet.

When students are ready, I slowly increase the complexity and number of options. For example, I might begin with a choice between two worksheets to practice addition or multiplication facts and then expand to a choice between using a worksheet, using flashcards, or reciting to a partner.

You can offer simple choices whenever you want to introduce a little variation in what children are doing or how they are doing it. When you regularly offer simple choices, you help children build a bank of experiences and develop their choice-making skills. With practice, students become better and better able to make good decisions about more complex options.

Teach basic routines to support independent work

In addition to making good choices, students need to know how to work independently. For students to do this, they need certain routines in place.

Routines that support Academic Choice include making the transition from meetings to independent work, gathering and returning supplies, getting help when needed, cleaning up at the end of a session, and moving chairs or tables to create work and meeting spaces.

Following is a discussion of how I might teach children routines for transitioning from the meeting area to working on independent tasks—you can use the same process to teach other routines.

Teaching a Routine

1. **Choose a "real-life" work activity but not an Academic Choice activity.**

2. **Model the routine.**

3. **Ask children what they observed.**

4. **Have several children model the routine followed by a discussion of observations.**

5. **Have everyone practice the routine while you observe and coach.**

6. **If needed, interrupt the work and review the procedures again.**

7. **Continue to pay attention to the routine during the next few independent work sessions.**

Choose a "real-life" work activity but not an Academic Choice activity

It is often helpful to put modeling in a "real-life" context. To do this, I use teacher assigned independent work, which I keep simple and brief. I make sure

**Teaching the
Skills Needed
for Success**

that the tasks are things that children can begin without my help because I am going to be busy observing and coaching their behavior. I do not use Academic Choice work because students need to know these routines before they engage in Academic Choice.

In this example, I've chosen a time when children will be working on an independent writing assignment where they will use the word wall or their student spelling dictionaries to help them with spelling.

Model the routine

Before they begin writing, I gather the children in a group on the meeting rug. I give them instructions for their writing task and then say, "We're going to talk about how to leave this space and get started with writing. Let's pretend I'm a student. I'm going to move from meeting time to writing time in a way that will help me do my best work. Watch me and see what you notice."

I first put my hand to my head to demonstrate thinking and look around the room. I carefully pick up a few pieces of writing paper from the storage bin and then walk over to the students' individual storage cubbies to get a spelling dictionary. (I have asked permission from a student to take a dictionary from her cubby.) I put the paper and student dictionary down at my desk, then pick up a pencil and take it to the pencil sharpener. After sharpening the pencil (pencil sharpening has been modeled and practiced earlier), I return to my desk and begin to write.

Ask children what they observed

"What did I do to get started on my writing?" I ask the group.

They respond with observations such as, "You sharpened your pencil before you sat down." "You thought about it before you got started." "You remembered to get the spelling dictionary."

"And how did I move about the room?" I ask.

"You were calm. You didn't run or anything," they respond. "You didn't stop and talk to anybody. You just got your things and sat down and started to work."

Have several children model the routine followed by a discussion of observations

I then ask for volunteers who want to demonstrate how to go from the meeting time to writing time. "Show us a helpful way to get started," I tell the first volunteer. We all watch silently as the child performs the same actions I did. He makes a point of pulling his chair out from the desk very quietly. We applaud when he is done, then I ask the children to name what he did that would help him do his best work.

Next, I ask three children to demonstrate the procedure at the same time. When the class has named what they did well, I issue a challenge. "Now you will *all* practice going from meeting time to writing time. What might be more challenging about all of us doing it at the same time?"

"It's harder not to bump into people."

"There might be a line at the pencil sharpener."

"It will be harder not to get distracted and talk to your friends."

Have everyone practice the routine while you observe and coach

I take a few suggestions from the group about how they could handle the challenges, then say, "When I give the signal, everyone will practice going from meeting time to writing time. I will watch and see how you do. Okay, time to get started on writing."

While the children practice making this transition, I stand back and observe, attempting to see what is going on in every part of the room. I want to reinforce positive behavior, and I choose my language carefully (see box on the next page):

"I see lots of people walking really calmly."

"I notice that some of you caught yourselves forgetting to get spelling dictionaries or move your chairs gently, then you remembered and took care of it."

"That was helpful, Angelo, when you picked up the pencil off the floor."

When I see children start to go off course, I assume they know the right thing to do and so I offer reminders:

"What do you need to be doing right now, Mirasia?"

"Show me a safe way to walk around the room, Andrew."

When a gentle reminder isn't enough, I redirect children toward the correct behavior:

"Kevin, go to your seat now."

"Kayla, get your paper and sit."

Teaching the Skills Needed for Success

Using Teacher Language to Encourage and Empower Children

The words a teacher uses and the way a teacher speaks have a powerful effect on children's social and academic learning. Through careful use of language, a teacher can encourage and empower children to live by classroom rules, to treat each other kindly, and to do their best learning.

At its best, teacher language:

- Is clear, simple, and direct

- Is specific and descriptive rather than general and evaluative

- Gives a clear indication of what the teacher expects from the child

- Shows faith that children can live by the rules

- Is genuine and respectful

Many teachers find it useful to categorize teacher language according to three purposes:

1. Language that reinforces children's positive efforts (*Marisa, I noticed you put the caps back on the markers after you used them. That will help them last longer.*)

2. Language that reminds children of the classroom rules and expectations (*Show me how you sit in the meeting circle.*)

3. Language that redirects children who begin to go off track (*Stephan, sit at your own table.*)

If needed, interrupt the work and review the procedures again

If I find myself giving lots of reminders and redirections, I'll stop midstream, even though this is happening during a writing lesson. Establishing smooth routines for transitions needs to be our focus. I give a pre-established (and practiced) signal to get students' immediate attention and ask them to return to the meeting area.

I might ask for their observations and share mine. I will definitely review my expectations for their behavior and have them try again. If a calm transition seems beyond their capabilities for now, we will go back to a more familiar way of working and try the transition again another day, perhaps with an opportunity to practice in small groups first.

Continue to pay attention to the routine
during the next few independent work sessions

Even if the class is successful at this first attempt at a whole group transition, I may want to have them practice it over the next few days while I coach. Whenever it's time for a transition, I remind the children that they are practicing, and I make a point of observing and coaching them. When transitions are going smoothly, I can teach a new routine, such as how to clean up, or how to get help on independent work. I also find it helpful to have the children reflect on how they are doing with transitions and what they could do to make them go even better.

Teach students how to do a variety of academic activities

Academic Choice can be one of the most peaceful and satisfying times of the day for both teachers and students. However, if Sara wants to make a crossword puzzle but isn't sure how to begin, Gerry and Ari need help thinking up ideas for their story, Kaysuan and Robert need advice on making a spelling dictionary, and their teacher is trying to be in three places at once, Academic Choice will be a lesson in frustration for everyone.

In addition to teaching routines, you'll want to be sure students have enough facility with each activity that you offer so that they can proceed with minimal supervision. Even though you may know that in past years students have made posters, written reports, made graphs, or engaged in any number of activities, you'll still want to allow time for review and practice.

Activities to teach or review will vary depending on the age of the students but might include:

- Making posters

- Writing reports

- Making graphs and diagrams

- Building dioramas

- Making mobiles

- Using graphic organizers to plan projects

- Writing poems and song lyrics

- Planning and acting out skits

- Drawing maps

**Teaching the
Skills Needed
for Success**

Following are a few ways you can help children learn how to do academic activities.

Teaching Students How to Do a Range of Academic Activities

- **Use already-established lessons**

- **Teach, model, and practice skills as needed**

- **Include activities that students do with special
area teachers**

Use already-established lessons to teach activities

Teaching or reviewing academic activities doesn't need to be a time-consuming add-on. You can use non-Academic Choice lessons to teach students skills they will need later in Academic Choice. During the early weeks of the school year, a first grade teacher taught her students how to keep track of data using tally marks, Venn diagrams, and pictographs. They practiced using these three methods to organize data in math lessons. Later, when the children were completing a science unit on sinking and floating, the teacher was able to offer the group a choice among these methods to record what items sank, floated, or both. The children were able to make informed choices and complete the tasks with independence because they had experience with each method.

A fourth grade teacher taught her students how to make acrostic poems during the first week of school as a language arts lesson and as a way to get to know each other better. They wrote their first name vertically and then wrote a phrase about themselves beginning with each of the letters. Later she taught other formats for writing poems such as diamantes and haiku. Once the children were familiar with these formats, she let them choose which format to use to write about the important traits of a book character. Before the children made their choices, she asked them what they remembered about each format and for a few examples of ways they might use each format to describe a character. Because they made their choices based on prior experiences with the different formats, most of the children were able to settle right into their work with a clear plan in mind. The teacher was able to have some wonderful conversations with students about using different forms of poetry to write about the characters.

Teach, model, and practice skills as needed

Teacher modeling followed by student practice while their teacher observes and coaches is a very effective strategy for teaching certain academic skills. For example, some Academic Choice lessons will ask children to do research and find out new information. In addition to using a dictionary, encyclopedia, and the Internet as research tools, children might want to conduct simple face-to-face or telephone interviews to gather information. Before sending children off to do interviews, I spend time teaching, modeling, and practicing interviewing techniques. For example, to teach students how to do phone interviews, we might spend time talking about how to formulate good questions, how to ask questions

politely, and how to take notes on the answers. They write a script and practice it with each other and with me before making the actual phone call.

Include activities that students do with special area teachers

Activity options might also include many activities that students learn to do with other teachers. A group that learned to sculpt with clay in art class was then able to do this activity as one of the options for creating a model animal habitat in science. Children who practiced making up new lyrics to simple and familiar songs in music class were able to use this strategy as an option for retelling a story from the days of the Pilgrims as part of an Academic Choice for a history lesson.

Teach students how to work collaboratively

Teaching the Skills Needed for Success

Finally, children will need to learn good collaborative work skills. I usually wait until children are comfortable with making group and individual choices and are able to enact those choices independently before I work on collaborative skills. When I'm ready to teach collaborative work skills, I use a two-step process. First, I teach children how to make decisions together with one other student. Then the partners work together to put their choice into action.

Teaching Collaborative Work Skills

- **Use paired decision making as a starting point**

- **Teach, model, and practice how to work together**

Use paired decision making as a starting point

To begin the process, I introduce a simple choice and assign each child to a partner. It is very important that children do not select their own partners while they are learning to work together, though there may well be times later in the year, when they are more experienced and Academic Choice lessons are running smoothly, when choosing partners or groups with whom to work could be an option.

Teacher and student model making a choice

To introduce the task and model the skills of collaboration, I enlist the help of one of the students and briefly plan what we might say before I begin the lesson.

Then, together we model making the choice as a pair in front of the class.

Here's how it might go:

The task is to choose among three topics (favorite colors, number of siblings, or favorite snacks of classmates) for gathering data and making bar graphs. I begin by stating my preference. "Favorite colors looks easiest," I say.

My accomplice models how to disagree. "Maybe," the student replies, "but I think it would be more interesting to see how many brothers and sisters people have. And that shouldn't be any harder than colors."

"No, I guess not," I reply, "but I had an idea about a way we could make the bar graph. We could use the colors to make the bars. The graph would look like a rainbow!"

"Oh, yeah, I like that idea. But maybe we could think of a good idea for a brothers' and sisters' graph, too."

"Hmmm." I furrow my brow. "Well, yeah, I guess the bars that show only brothers could be blue and only sisters could be pink and both brothers and sisters could be purple. Oooh! I like that! Blue, pink, and purple. Do you want to do that? Brothers and sisters and make the graph like that?" I ask.

"Okay. Then you get to have a graph you like and I get to do the topic I wanted."

Students discuss what they observed

When we finish this scene, I ask the class what they noticed. The students comment that we disagreed and that we both stated the reasons for our choices.

"Yes," I say, "we had to know what each other was thinking before we could decide together."

They also note that we didn't argue and that we were able to combine our ideas.

"I might have been tempted to just insist on doing the favorite colors because I really liked my idea," I say. "How might my partner feel if I did that?"

"Mad, because you didn't care what he wanted to do."

"Probably! But instead we found a way to do the part I liked and the part about brothers and sisters that my partner liked. We were able to decide on our own without anyone's help."

Students practice paired decision making

At this point, I announce the list of partners and send children off to discuss their ideas and come to a decision about which of the three topics they will use for the assignment. I stand back at first to see how the group is doing and then begin to circulate so I can observe and coach individual pairs.

**Teaching the
Skills Needed
for Success**

My goal with a modeling procedure such as this is to show students a way to reach agreement despite beginning with different choices. Sharing the reasons behind our choices and then finding compromise is one strategy for doing this. Another strategy could be agreeing to one person's choice with the stipulation that the other person will get his or her way another time.

Students are often able to propose other possibilities, especially after they have a little experience with working as partners. It is not necessary to model all the possibilities—students get the idea and generalize when they see one possibility modeled clearly.

Teach, model, and practice how to work together

Once students have made and reported their decisions, my accomplice and I take a few minutes to model a way to work together collaboratively. Here's what we might say in the data-gathering example:

"Let's see. There are twenty-six kids in the class including us. So we can each ask twelve kids," I propose to my partner.

"Do we ask each other how many brothers and sisters we have, or just write it down in our own notes?"

"Let's ask each other. That's more fun!" I say. "But how will I know who you've already asked? We have to be sure we get everybody once."

"Let's write down everyone's names. Then we'll divide the list in half. You ask your half and I'll ask my half."

"Good idea!" I say.

Students discuss their observations, share ideas, and reflect on the process

I ask the class what they noticed. After they report their observations, I might ask what other ideas they have for sharing the work fairly and getting it done with accuracy, or I might simply send them off to work, then observe and coach them.

Once they've completed the assignment, I'll hold a brief reflection meeting where I ask them to think about what went well and what they could do better.

Once children are able to work productively in pairs, I can use the same procedures to teach them to work collaboratively in small groups, if future lessons will call for that. Collaborating with several people at once is more difficult than collaborating with just one, as many of us know from experience! The skills gained from first working in pairs will carry over to group work, but children will also need some additional modeling and practice.

The next step

When children have learned these basic skills—making decisions, following basic routines, independently doing a variety of academic activities, and collaborating productively—they are well on their way to being able to engage in simple Academic Choice experiences. An important next step is learning how to use a variety of classroom materials independently and creatively. To help them do this, teachers can use a process called Guided Discovery, which I present in depth in the next chapter.

Chapter Two

GUIDED DISCOVERY

In Guided Discovery, children use observation, brainstorming, and exploratory play to learn about the use and care of materials. Guided Discovery is an essential part of preparing children for Academic Choice. A typical Guided Discovery lasts approximately thirty minutes. In that time, children not only learn how to use materials that they'll need for Academic Choice, they also gain practice in thinking independently and critically, generating and carrying out plans, engaging deeply with their work, solving problems, and learning from each other.

There are five steps in a Guided Discovery:

1. Introduction and naming of materials
2. Generating and modeling of students' ideas
3. Exploration and experimentation
4. Sharing exploratory work
5. Cleanup and care of materials

First, children take a close look at the material and review what they already know about its use. Then they generate new ideas about how they might use the material in school. A few children model one or more of the ideas and then everyone has a chance to try out some of the ideas. Children share the results of their explorations with each other and the teacher through a brief, structured discussion that encourages them to reflect on what they accomplished, how they did it, and problems they encountered. Seeing and hearing about each other's experiences expands the repertoire of all the children in the group. In addition to introducing materials, teachers might use Guided Discovery to introduce children to independent use of classroom libraries, school libraries, writing centers, or playground equipment.

In the following pages, you'll read about a Guided Discovery done in a primary grade classroom along with my commentary on the teacher's process. I follow this with a Guided Discovery of the same material done in an upper elementary classroom. Since the upper elementary classroom example highlights any variations that might occur, I encourage teachers to read the primary grade example first.

Open-ended vs. recitation questions in Guided Discoveries

Guided Discovery

As you read the examples, pay attention to the kinds of questions the teachers ask. Asking questions is an important part of Guided Discovery, particularly open-ended questions. Open-ended questions are those for which any reasoned and relevant response is a correct response. The goal of open-ended questioning is to stimulate thinking and encourage creative exploration. For example, if I want children to think about the best way to store markers, I might ask, "How could we put away these markers so that they will be kept in good condition?" I receive all relevant and sincere responses with equal endorsement. Children might suggest that they each keep a set of markers in their desks, that they put them all in a large container behind the teacher's desk, that they keep them in their original boxes, or any number of responses that I could not predict in advance.

However, there might be times when I want a specific answer or set of answers. For example, if I have already shown the children where and how I want the markers stored and I want to jog their memories, I would ask a recitation question, "Where do the markers go when we are not using them?" This question acknowledges that there is an established place for markers and alerts the children that I am looking for a particular answer.

Problems will arise if I ask an open-ended question when I really want students to recite a correct answer. For example, I might have a very clear idea of the best container for the markers. But I'm trying to use open-ended questions in my teaching so instead of showing the children where to store the markers, I ask, "How could we put these markers away so that…" Unintentionally, I've asked a manipulative question that undermines the goals of Guided Discovery. Here's how the conversation might go:

Paula: How could we put these markers away so that they will stay in good condition? Seven students raise their hands.

Student: We could keep them in our desks.

*Paula: Oh. Well, we **could**, but then your desks will be more cluttered.*

Student: You could keep them in the teacher's closet. They'd be safe there.

Paula: Yeah, but then I'd have to stop and get them for you. I want you to get them yourselves when you need them. C'mon, who sees what we can do?

Most of the raised hands are down now.

The children quickly recognize that I don't want their thoughts; I want them to guess my thoughts. Sharing ideas becomes too risky because they can see that I don't value their ideas. Clearly I want them to tell me something that they seem to be too dumb to know. I would have been better off simply showing them where to store the markers when they were still excited about using them.

In Appendix B, you'll find a script for a Guided Discovery. Many teachers find this script useful to guide them through the steps and prompt them to use open-ended questions. But remember there might be times when a recitation question or a demonstration will better fit your time frame and goals.

Step 1: Introduction and naming of materials

(Approximate time: five minutes)

In step 1, teachers will want to:

- **Generate interest and stimulate thinking**

- **Acknowledge children's expertise**

- **Generate a common vocabulary**

- **Encourage close observation**

Generate interest and stimulate thinking

Ms. Martell has gathered the first graders in a circle in the meeting area. She holds a small covered opaque plastic container.

"I have some wonderful tools in this box," she says as she shakes the box. "These tools come in many colors. Who has a guess what they could be?"

"Legos?" guesses Tony.

"Crayons!"

**Guided
Discovery**

"Toys!"

"Yes, this could be any of those tools," Ms. Martell says. "I'll give you another clue. You use these tools to draw."

"It's got to be markers or crayons," says Raisha.

"It could be colored pencils. I have some of those and you draw with them too," says Jasmine.

"It's one of those three things. Let's see which one," Ms. Martell says as she slowly opens the container and pulls out a box with a flourish.

"Markers! It's markers!" the children gleefully shout.

Since markers are a familiar tool, Ms. Martell wanted the children to view them with fresh eyes, so she created a mystery about what was in the box, encouraging children to drop preconceptions and engage their thinking.

In addition to creating a mystery, Ms. Martell held the container with reverence. She called its contents "wonderful tools." She opened the box and revealed the markers with a dramatic flourish. Everything about her introduction communicated that these markers were a delightful addition to their classroom.

Notice that Ms. Martell did not tell the children if their guesses about the contents of the box were right or wrong. Instead, she commented on their thinking ("It could have been any of those things") and gave a further clue. The goal was to stimulate their thinking and curiosity, not to get a correct guess. Therefore, each response was equal in value.

If the children seemed to struggle with this challenge, or many of their guesses seemed off base, this might indicate that they have little experience with this kind of thinking. In that case, the teacher could model the process by making a guess herself and explaining why she made it. For example, she might say, "These tools could be counters like we use in math because I know those come in different colors. What else do we have in our class that comes in different colors?"

If a teacher thinks there are just a few children who have difficulty making reasoned guesses, she might ask children to explain why they made their guesses. Those who are less skilled can learn from their classmates how to make "educated" guesses rather than random ones. Over time, more and more children will contribute ideas.

Acknowledge children's expertise

Ms. Martell gently shakes the markers out on a carpet square in front of her. "What do you know about markers?" she asks.

The children eagerly raise their hands. They tell her that they can draw pictures with markers or decorate their writing. They can make signs and color. They can make cards for people.

Ms. Martell's open-ended question, "What do you know about markers?" validated children's expertise and encouraged the children to think for themselves. Since only they know how they have used markers before, any sincere answer is a correct answer. And when children believe that their thoughts will be valued rather than judged, they are willing to put their energy into thinking.

Generate a common vocabulary

Anika remarks that she likes the pink markers the best. Ms. Martell follows up on this by asking, "What are some of the colors of the markers we have here?"

The children name the colors with ease until Isaac hesitates and then says, "I don't know the name but it's kind of a greeny blue."

"Yes, that's a very accurate description, Isaac. The name that they call that color is aqua."

Ms. Martell wanted to be sure the children knew the names of the colors that might be less familiar to them. If Anika or another child had not mentioned color names, Ms. Martell might have asked the children what colors they saw or what colors they could name.

Because Ms. Martell wanted children to draw on their prior knowledge, she asked them to name what they saw, rather than asking them to guess the name on the marker barrel. When Isaac described the aqua marker as greeny blue, Ms. Martell was able to endorse his powers of description and his knowledge of colors and then simply state the name on the barrel of the marker for their information.

Encourage close observation

Ms. Martell carries the set of markers around the circle so that each child can get a close look. "What are some other things you might say to describe what these markers look like?" she asks.

The children notice that they are all the same size and that they have the name of the color written on them. "The color on the side is the same as the color it draws," observes Lorna.

Guided Discovery

"Yes, that's true. We can call that part of the marker that holds the ink inside it the barrel," Ms. Martell tells the class. She removes the top of the marker and points. *"This part is called the tip. What do you notice about the tip?"*

"It's kind of flat on one side, but on the other side it's kind of pointy."

"That's a careful observation, Kyle," she says. *"I wonder why they made it that shape? Let's keep thinking about that."*

Ms. Martell hadn't planned to give the children the name for the barrel of the marker, but when it came up in the discussion, she knew that having that term would help the children talk about the markers with more clarity.

Ms. Martell wanted the class to pay attention to the tip of the marker because the shape of the tip affects the kinds of lines that students can draw. If a student had not pointed out the shape of the tip, Ms. Martell would have made the observation herself. But instead of elaborating on the impact of the tip's shape, she asked a question: "I wonder why it's like that?" She didn't expect an answer because she knows that sometimes, unanswered questions generate more thinking than answered ones.

Step 2: Generating and modeling of ideas

(Approximate time: five minutes)

In step 2, teachers will want to:

- **Use open-ended questions to stimulate thinking**

- **Decide when to chart the ideas**

- **Use the students' own words**

- **Emphasize student modeling**

- **Challenge students to stretch their thinking**

Use open-ended questions to stimulate thinking

"What can we do with these markers to help us with our learning? Let's see how many good ideas we can think of," Ms. Martell says.

Ms. Martell's goal was to stimulate thinking, so she began with an open-ended question. As the first students shared ideas, others listened. These ideas often triggered other ideas and momentum grew along with the children's thinking. When teachers are open to a range of responses, students feel free to take risks in their thinking and share ideas.

Decide whether to chart the ideas

Ms. Martell picks up a marker and prepares to write the children's ideas on chart paper.

"We can draw pictures," Rose announces.

"Yes, we can!" responds Ms. Martell, who then writes "draw pictures" on the chart.

At any age, seeing one's thoughts in print is affirming and encouraging. For beginning readers, this is also a teaching strategy. They know what the words say (in general, at least) because they said them. The connection between words and print, and perhaps more importantly between personal meaning and print, is reinforced. In addition, the list serves as a reminder of different things the children can try when they begin to work with the materials.

Guided Discovery

However, writing the children's ideas down is not necessary for a good Guided Discovery. In fact, there are times when it makes more sense not to list ideas. Writing ideas on a chart takes a lot of time, and young children, in particular, might become restless. Each teacher will need to decide when to write down children's ideas and when to simply listen.

Use the students' own words

"What might you put in a picture, Rose?"

"Ummm . . . I like to draw me and my mom and my sisters."

"If I write 'families' will that tell your idea?"

"Yes," Rose responds, so Ms. Martell writes "families" as a subcategory of "draw pictures."

We often feel a need to save both time and space as we record ideas. Ms. Martell summarized Rose's idea but was careful to check in with Rose before rephrasing to be sure she had gotten Rose's essential meaning.

I know I am sometimes tempted to rephrase students' words without a check-in. I have even caught myself responding to a student's idea with "Oh that gives me an idea!" then writing my own idea rather than the student's idea. This can kill good brainstorming! I certainly might include an idea or two of my own along with those of students, but I avoid doing so in place of a student's idea.

Emphasize student modeling

"Rose, would you show us how you might draw someone in your family?" Ms. Martell asks. Rose agrees and comes to sit next to Ms. Martell, who hands her the container of markers and some drawing paper attached to a clipboard.

Rose selects a brown marker and removes the cap, placing the cap on the floor. She begins to draw.

"What do you notice?" Ms. Martell asks the group.

"She's making a person."

"She looked in the markers and picked brown for the body."

After completing the outline of the body, Rose replaces the cap on the brown marker, puts it back in the container, and selects a blue marker, which she uses to draw a dress on the person. Once again, students voice their observations.

Ms. Martell says, "You are really noticing some important things about how Rose is using the markers. Someone also noticed that she put the brown marker back in the basket when she was done with it. What else do you notice about how she's taking care of the markers while she works?"

"She put the cap back on when she was finished."

"She's only taking out one marker at a time."

Rose replaces the cap on the blue marker and returns it to the container.

"Okay, thank you, Rose. You gave us some good ideas and you took good care of the markers. I have a trick that will help you all keep up with the caps so that they don't get lost when you use a marker." Ms. Martell selects a marker, removes the cap, and makes a show of popping it on the back end of the marker. "What did I do?"

"You put the cap on the other end."

"Yes, and did you hear it make a snapping noise?" She pulls the cap off and snaps it on again. "That snap is how I know it's on good and tight. Now, what else might we draw pictures of?" The children share ideas for drawing pictures of school, their houses, animals, friends, dinosaurs, snakes, flowers, and trees.

Liam volunteers to model his idea of drawing a cat. Snapping the cap on the end of the marker, he draws an orange cat and then outlines it in black so that it shows up better.

"What can you tell me about how Liam is holding the marker? Look carefully," Ms. Martell says.

The children notice that he is holding it at a slant.

"Yes, that helps him press down more gently," she tells them. "What might happen to the marker if Liam presses hard?"

"It would be too dark."

"It would smoosh the pointy part."

"Yes, it's easy to mess up a drawing or a marker that way," Ms. Martell remarks.

Ms. Martell had the students do most of the modeling because she wanted them to demonstrate that they could use the markers on their own. If she had wanted students to use tools in a particular way, she would have modeled the tool use herself. During the first days of school, she modeled how to grip and

Chapter Two

write with a pencil. She modeled how to hold and carry scissors and how to use them to cut out pictures for a phonics exercise.

However, in this Guided Discovery, she was confident that the student modelers would demonstrate the proper care of the markers. If they forgot an important detail, Ms. Martell could briefly model it again as she did with the demonstration of snapping the cap on the back end of the marker.

She also wanted students to learn from each other. As the student modelers approached this creative task, they demonstrated how to make decisions when a task is open-ended. This gave children some very concrete ideas that could help them get started on their own explorations.

Challenge students to stretch their thinking

**Guided
Discovery**

"You have lots of ideas and I bet you'll think of even more. What could we do with the markers besides draw pictures?"

No hands go up immediately. After a moment, Ms. Martell tells the group, "I remember someone said they had made signs with markers before, so I'll add that to the list."

Two hands go up and the children add "writing with markers" and "decorating their writing." "We're off to a great start. I wonder if we can come up with one more idea that we haven't thought of yet." Ms. Martell looks around the circle thoughtfully.

"Designs. We could make a design with the markers," Anika offers.

"Anika, would you like to show us how you might get started making a design with the markers?"

Anika looks the markers over and picks up a purple one. She draws a large circle and then switches to a pink marker for smaller circles. Ms. Martell calls on children for their observations.

"She picked purple and pink," one child says.

"Did anybody notice how Anika was able to make some of her lines thick and some thin?" asks the teacher.

"It was how she held the marker," Justin points out. "The fat lines are from holding it so that it draws with the flat side."

"Thank you, Anika. You gave us some good ideas."

Ms. Martell also challenged students to go beyond their first ideas. Once children had generated a long list of ideas for drawing pictures, a familiar use of markers, she suggested another category to think about. When they seemed stuck, she gave an example that helped them make new associations and think of new ideas. Then, she challenged them further. "I wonder if we can come up with one more idea that we haven't thought of yet."

Her language made the challenge fun, rather than stressful. By saying "I wonder . . ." Ms. Martell implied that if they couldn't think of another idea, it was okay.

Step 3: Exploration and experimentation

(Approximate time: ten to fifteen minutes)

In step 3, teachers will want to:

- **Plan for a smooth transition**

- **Plan open-ended but limited tasks that encourage children to learn from each other**

- **Observe children as they work**

Plan for a smooth transition

"Now you will all have a chance to try out some ideas for using the markers," Ms. Martell tells the children. "I'm going to give each of you two markers and some drawing paper."

She gives each child a clipboard, drawing paper that has lines drawn on it to divide it into four sections, and two markers of different colors.

Ms. Martell could have had the children return to their seats before beginning their exploration but she chose to have them stay in the circle. The children were excited and ready to work. The transition back to their seats might have been difficult and taken a lot of time, plus it might have interrupted their excitement.

Plan open-ended but limited tasks that encourage children to learn from each other

Once all the children have the supplies, Ms. Martell tells them, "In one of the boxes on your drawing paper, make a picture of someone in your family like Rose suggested."

The children draw. After she can see that most have completed their drawings, she tells them, "If you'd like to share your drawing, you can hold it up now. Let's look and see all the different ways you drew people."

Most of the children hold up their drawings. As they look around, they see a variety of ways to draw people.

"Now in another box on your paper, do some writing with your markers like Tom did," Ms. Martell says.

**Guided
Discovery**

Upper elementary students explore watercolors.

Once again the children busy themselves with the markers. "I see lots of good ideas for making letters with markers," their teacher tells them. "I see lots of different letters and words." After they've had a chance to make a few letters, the children are once again invited to hold their work up for others to see. This time, Ms. Martell asks them, "Who sees a good idea that someone else had for writing with markers?"

"Joe used both markers so the letters all have two different colored lines."

"It looks like Karina wrote script!"

"Martin made his letter real big."

"Now in a new box, make a design like Anika suggested," Ms. Martell instructs, and the children make designs and share them. Finally, Ms. Martell tells the children, "In the last box, try out an idea of your own."

The children now begin to produce many different kinds of drawings from abstract designs to pictures. Karina goes back to trying to write in script, and several other children do so as well. Others draw monsters, shapes, swirling lines, or trees, grass, and sky. Two children share their markers so that they can make rainbows with four colors instead of only two.

Ms. Martell gave the children tasks that were open-ended yet limited. She began by asking them to use the markers in a familiar way, drawing people. This way they could begin with confidence. She then moved on to ideas that were newer and perhaps riskier. Because the tasks were also open-ended (i.e., there are lots of ways to draw people or make letters or a design), the children drew upon their own resources for ideas and perhaps those of each other, but did not need to turn to Ms. Martell. She also encouraged children to share their work so that they could learn from each other.

Observe children as they work

While the children work, Ms. Martell circulates among them. She asks questions that will help her understand how the children are thinking and makes suggestions if one of them seems stuck. But mostly she observes them as they work.

"I notice that many of you are trying out both the pointy edge and the wide edge of your markers," she announces to the group at one point. "It will be fun to see what kinds of things you can do with the different edges."

"I see so many different kinds of ideas," she tells them a few minutes later. "There is lots of good thinking going on here. We have three more minutes before it's time to share. It's okay if you don't finish. Just get to a good stopping place."

Though the children were now deeply engaged in drawing, and she was simply overseeing them, Ms. Martell worked just as hard during this part of the Guided Discovery as she did during the introduction when she led the meeting. Some of the most intense work occurred when she appeared to be simply sitting and watching, not engaging with her students. Her observations gave her a lot of information about her students and allowed her to encourage and empower them through her use of language. This feedback supported them in their efforts to work with creativity and independence.

Step 4: Sharing exploratory work

(Approximate time: five minutes)

In step 4, teachers will want to:

- **Ask for volunteers to share**

- **Give children a variety of ways to share their work**

- **Structure the sharing to help students respond positively and usefully to each other's work**

Ask for volunteers to share

Ms. Martell rings a chime to get children's attention.

"It's time to put your work down and get ready to talk about what you've done and learned." She waits until all children are quiet and focused. "Now who would like to tell us one thing they like about their drawing? We have time for three people to share."

Many hands go up.

Sharing work is always voluntary. Most children are eager to share, but some children won't feel good about what they've done. The medium may be unfamiliar or awkward for them, they may have gotten stuck on their first idea and started over from scratch, they may be shy, or they may simply be having a tough day. If the children are to feel free to truly experiment and try out new ideas, they need to know that they will not be required to share their work if they don't want to.

Guided Discovery

Give children a variety of ways to share their work

Ms. Martell selects among the children whose drawings were not recognized during step 3. Kevin holds his design up in front of him and tells the class that he likes the colors he used. Marisa likes the way she made an AB pattern. Renee tells the class that she likes the way she made her drawing.

This meeting was not the only opportunity for children to share what they were doing. During the previous step, Ms. Martell paused after each task and asked students to hold up their work if they wanted to. Having everyone display their work at the same time lowered the risk factor and increased the number of children who were willing to share what they'd done.

Although all the children can hold their work up for display, if they wish, only a few share verbally in any one sharing session. Over time, with Guided Discoveries of other classroom materials, all the children who want such recognition will have it. It is not necessary for all to have their work discussed in one session.

Structure the sharing to help students respond positively and usefully to each other's work

Renee's comment about her work is general, so Ms. Martell asks her, "What's one thing you like about your drawing?" With this encouragement, Renee says, "I like the colors I used."

Stimulating thinking and reflection is one of the central goals of a sharing meeting, but students often don't know how to think about their own work or respond to each other with helpful questions and comments. Instead, they tend to make general comments such as, "I like my drawing," "I like what Rose did," or "Anthony's design is cool!" These sorts of comments are based on feelings rather than careful observation, thinking, and reflection. Ms. Martell's question not only prompted Renee to think more deeply about her process but also modeled for the children a way of thinking about their own work and responding to each other's work.

In step 3, Ms. Martell asked an open-ended question to guide children's comments on each other's work: *"Who sees a good idea that someone else had for writing with markers?"* By asking for specific, positive information, she maintained emotional safety and helped the children expand their knowledge of ways to use markers.

Here are some other phrases teachers can use to encourage specific and positive reflection:

- Tell one thing you discovered about . . .

- Tell about a strategy you used to . . .

- What was the hardest part?

- What was the most interesting part?

- What surprised you?

Step 5: Cleanup and care of materials

(Approximate time: five minutes)

In step 5, teachers will want to:

- **Ask students to model routines for cleanup and care**

- **Structure whole-group cleanup to meet the group's needs**

Ask students to model routines for cleanup and care

Guided Discovery

"It's time to clean up and get ready for math. Now that you have practiced using the markers, they will be kept on our art shelves so that you can get them whenever you need to use them." Ms. Martell walks over to a set of shelves on a wall beneath a row of windows and points to an empty part of a shelf. "I've cleared this space and we'll keep all the containers here from now on. Who will show us a responsible way to put away a set of markers on this shelf after using them?"

Miguel volunteers. He picks up a set of markers replacing caps on some of them that need it. Once he has them in his hand, he places them in an empty container, walks over to the art shelves, and places the container of markers in the designated area.

"Thank you, Miguel. How many things can you name that Miguel did to clean up and take care of our markers?" Ms. Martell looks around the group while Miguel returns proudly to the circle.

"He put all the caps back on."

"He walked."

"He made sure he had one of every color in the box."

"He put them in the right place on the shelf."

Ms. Martell smiles. "You noticed a lot of important things."

As in step 2, the children took responsibility for modeling. Ms. Martell prepared them for this. Early in the year, she modeled procedures for clearing markers off tables and returning them to their containers. By the time she did this Guided Discovery, she had shown the class where she wanted the markers to be stored, and she was confident that Miguel could model an appropriate way to clean up and put away the markers.

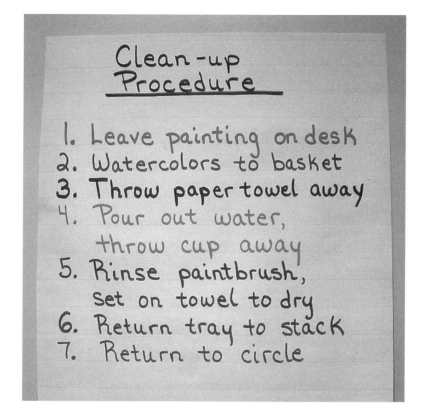

Structure whole-group cleanup to meet the group's needs

Ms. Martell follows up on Miguel's demonstration by saying, "When I give the signal, everyone will clean up their markers. I will watch. When everyone is sitting at clean tables, I'll know you are ready for math."

Ms. Martell stands and observes the children as they put away the markers. As she did during their exploratory time, she provides feedback. Once all the students are seated at tables, she begins the math lesson.

With their classmate's leadership, and the coaching of their teacher, the rest of the children were prepared to conduct cleanup independently. Teachers who are concerned that their students are not ready to conduct such a cleanup as a whole group may want to have table groups clean up while the other children observe, until the routines are well established.

Guided Discovery with older students

Since Guided Discovery is all about introducing materials and work areas, it might seem as though Guided Discovery is most appropriate for young children for whom everything is new. But older children also benefit from Guided Discoveries. There are several important reasons why this is so.

- Not all children have had equal exposure to materials such as scissors, glue, construction paper, markers, crayons, calculators, or rulers. Guided Discoveries help establish a common knowledge base and enable all students to begin using the materials with confidence, care, and enjoyment.

- For children, it's easy to forget newly learned knowledge and skills during the long summer vacation. Just as children need time to review content learned in past years, they need time to review ways to use classroom materials, especially if they are to use them in creative ways.

Guided Discovery

- You can use Guided Discovery to help older children think about creative uses for familiar materials. I recently observed a Guided Discovery of hole punches in a fifth grade classroom. The children brainstormed an impressive range of ideas for using this simple tool in their Academic Choice work. For example, they could use the hole punch (along with other materials) to make little books, mobiles, paper or cardboard objects with moving parts, spinners for games, pictures and letters made with patterns of holes, and pictures or patterns made with the dots created when holes are punched.

- Guided Discoveries provide opportunities for teachers to establish their own expectations for use and care of materials, which may be different from the expectations of teachers that children have had in the past. Guided Discoveries also allow teachers and children to interact in ways that help them get to know and enjoy each other.

Although the basic procedure is the same at any age, in older grades teachers may focus more on the development of creativity and thinking skills and somewhat less on basic procedures than they do for younger children.

Following is a step-by-step example of a Guided Discovery of markers done in a fifth grade classroom. My discussion highlights the ways in which this Guided Discovery differs from the Guided Discovery of markers done with primary grade students. The example and discussion will be most useful if you read the primary grade example first.

Step 1: Introduction and naming of materials

It can be more challenging to generate thoughtful interest in materials such as markers when students have used them as standard classroom supplies for several years. In the following example, fifth grade teacher Ms. Wells moves quickly through the introduction and naming step, skipping the mystery building introduction altogether.

Ms. Wells holds a canister full of various colors of markers, one of several containers that she recently placed on the classroom supply shelves.

"Some of you might have noticed that the markers are out on the shelves now," she says to the circle of students. "As of today, they will be available for you to use as you need them. I'm sure most of you have a lot of experience using markers. In fact, you're probably getting to be something like experts! So let's celebrate having the use of all these beautiful markers by hearing some of your collective wisdom. What do you know about them?"

"I know that if you try to color in a really big space with one color it gets used up. Paint works lots better for big areas," Rachael shares.

"True. Does anybody know why that happens?" asks Ms. Wells.

"Well there's only so much ink in the barrel. Markers are good for outlining things and coloring in small areas," Micah answers.

Many students raise their hands, and Ms. Wells continues to call on children for ideas.

"The tip of a yellow marker gets other colors on it if you draw over them, and then it doesn't make a really clear yellow any more."

"If you go over blue with yellow you get green."

"I know that you can draw lines thin or thick depending on how you hold the marker."

Ms. Wells used voice tone and words to convey excitement about the "beautiful markers." Asking children to share their wisdom acknowledged their expertise and built their sense of competence. As they eagerly remembered past experiences and shared their thoughts, the fifth graders also increased their common awareness and knowledge of the markers.

**Chapter
Two**

Step 2: Generating and modeling of ideas

With older children, starting from a base of familiarity helps children generate new ideas. Wanting to keep the momentum going, Ms. Wells lists all the ideas before asking any student to model.

"Out of all the ways you've used markers in the past, what are some of your favorites?" asks Ms. Wells.

"I like illustrating the stories I write with them," offers Tamika.

Other students tell about how they used to love to make scribble pictures and mazes with markers. They report making thank you cards and valentines; lettering for signs, patterns, illustrated reports; and the background scenes for dioramas.

"That's a lot of ideas!" Ms. Wells says. "But now I have a challenge for you. How many new ideas can you think of for using markers this year in fifth grade? Take a minute to think. You may talk to a neighbor about ideas if you'd like."

After a short discussion period, the children share their ideas.

"We could make pictures or drawings to show fractions."

"Decorate our folders."

"Make a game board."

"You could make sets of cards with something about each state! Or people we learn about in history."

"You're really thinking!" says Ms. Wells enthusiastically. "I had an idea too. You could use the markers to make really beautiful maps."

"Let's see. We've got some interesting ideas up here," Ms. Wells says looking at the list on the chart. "I wonder how you might begin to make a game board. Who can show us a way to begin that?"

Guided Discovery

Ramon raises his hand quickly. "Let's see how Ramon goes about this," Ms. Wells says. "Watch carefully, and we'll see how many details you remember."

Ramon takes a black marker from the canister, removes the cap from its tip, and snaps the cap on the back end. As he gets ready to draw, he asks if he can use a ruler, which he uses to draw two parallel straight lines, then horizontal lines between the two to make individual squares. Putting the ruler down he continues the parallel lines but makes them curve until they point back in the direction from which they began. He then uses the ruler to make individual squares in this section.

"Okay, that's a good start, Ramon," Ms. Wells tells him. "Keep working on your game board and let's hear what people notice." Hands raise.

"He used a ruler to make the lines straight, but then he just made the curvy part without a ruler."

"He's holding the marker gently so the lines are real thin."

"It looks like he's making all the squares about the same size."

As Ramon continues to work, he begins to color the first square blue, then the second one red.

"He's filling in the squares with different colors, so it's easy to tell them apart," says Liv.

"When he colors, he holds the markers more on the side, so it fills in the square quicker."

"When he finished using a marker, he put the cap back on and put it away."

"Okay, thanks for that demonstration, Ramon." Ms. Wells tells him. "Did anyone notice the things Ramon was doing to take care of the markers besides putting the cap back when he was done?"

"When he used them to color, he only colored the little squares. He didn't try to color a huge space."

"Yeah, and he didn't bear down real hard with them and mess up the point on the tip."

"He's putting all of them back in the container."

Rather than having several children model different aspects of marker use, Ms. Wells had one child model a more complex idea. The children already knew how to use and care for markers. Ramon indirectly provided a review as he worked on making the game board. In addition to a brief refresher, the children were able to see one approach to implementing a new idea.

Asking another child to model a different idea would have demonstrated some different strategies and reinforced the basic care of the markers further. But Ms. Wells felt that the children had been sitting long enough and they needed a chance to try the markers for themselves. The children were alert and thinking. Holding them for too long and trying to make too many points could have diminished their enthusiasm.

Chapter Two

Step 3: Exploration and experimentation

For the fifth graders in Ms. Wells's classroom, this is a less structured experience than for the first graders. The children do their exploring back at their tables rather than on the rug, and they can choose to explore any of the ideas listed during the brainstorming session.

"Now you will have some time to try out some of your favorite ideas while you practice using the markers," Ms. Wells tells the class. "There are enough sets of markers for each table group to have one. You know where the drawing paper is. We have about fifteen minutes. I'll dismiss you by table groups."

While Ms. Wells observes, the children gather markers and paper and quickly settle at their tables. Many are discussing their ideas with each other. "I see some of you are helping each other get ideas about what to do."

Mike is wandering. She watches him for a moment and sees him go over to another table to talk to a friend. "Michael, where do you need to be right now?" she asks him. He points to his table and returns to it.

Overall, the children are already very focused. Most have begun to draw. Ms. Wells walks over to Aron, who seems to be having a hard time getting started. "How's it going?" she asks him.

"Okay, I guess. I want to do something different from usual, but I just don't know what to draw," he answers.

After a brief conversation, Ms. Wells tells him about a book in the class library that might give him some ideas about designs to draw.

She looks in on Marie and Hannah. Marie is slowly drawing shapes that look like paisley. She finishes a blue one, then picks up a yellow marker and begins to color in the shape. Hannah's design looks very much like Marie's.

"My sister loves paisley," Marie tells her teacher. "I thought it would be fun to see if I could draw it. It's kind of complicated."

"Great challenge! Some paisley patterns have lots of smaller patterns within the larger ones," Ms. Wells tells her. "I'll be interested to see how you make yours."

"You've got lots of good ideas," she tells the group after a while. "We have three more minutes before it's time to bring your work back to the rug to share."

**Guided
Discovery**

Ms. Wells drew on a familiar routine—dismissing students by table groups—to help ensure a smooth transition. And because she and the students had worked on other classroom routines, such as getting supplies independently, she could trust students to settle down quickly and quietly to their task. Working at their tables gave them the space they needed to try out some of their more complex ideas. However, if time had been a concern, they could have worked in the meeting circle as the first graders did.

Ms. Wells's primary task during this time was to observe and guide when necessary. Throughout the fifteen-minute exploration time, Ms. Wells circulated among the children. She asked questions that would help her understand how the children were thinking and made suggestions like the one she made for Aron if one of them seemed stuck. Almost all of them were decidedly NOT stuck, however. They were drawing intensely. She also reinforced their good work, reminded them about behavior guidelines, and redirected them if their behavior started to get off track.

Step 4: Sharing exploratory work

Since students have been working away from the circle, Ms. Wells needs to allow time for them to gather in the circle again. She structures the sharing so that everyone has a chance to reflect on their process and talk about this with one other person.

When the fifteen-minute exploratory time is up, Ms. Wells calls the children back to the meeting rug where they, once again, sit in a circle. "If you would like us to see your work, put it out on the floor in front of you," she tells them. All but two children place their work on the floor. "*Let's take a minute and look around at all the different kinds of projects we have here. There are so many good ideas! Without talking, just look and see how many different ideas you can see.*"

There is a moment of silence as the children look. After a moment, Ms. Wells asks, "Who would like to share one good idea that they noticed?"

"*Ramon's picture is awesome!*" *Terence says.*

"*What do you see on his design that makes it awesome, Terence?*" *interjects Ms. Wells.*

"*It looks like lots of lightning bolts.*"

"*Hannah and Marie's designs are pretty,*" *Marcel says.*

"*What is pretty about them?*" *Ms. Wells prompts.*

"*They kept using yellow to color it in, but the outlines are all different colors.*"

"*Even though you are practically experts on markers, they are pretty amazing tools, and there is always something new to learn about them,*" *Ms. Wells says.* "*Can you think of something you learned about markers today that you didn't know before? Or did you remember something about them that you had forgotten? Just think without talking for a minute.*"

The children sit quietly. After a moment, Ms. Wells continues, "Now turn to a neighbor and take turns sharing something new you learned or something important that you remembered about the markers."

As the children share, Ms. Wells catches bits of conversations. Someone remembered how easy it is to lose the caps, another that it works best to outline a shape before coloring it in. One boy tells another that he figured out how to draw grass so that it really looks like there are individual blades, and his partner responds that he got some good ideas about how to make fancy letters for book covers and posters.

This sharing session helped extend children's thinking as they learned from each other's good ideas. Ms. Wells encouraged this learning by asking specific focus questions. A challenge for upper elementary teachers and students is believing that there really is more to learn about simple tools. The way in which Ms. Wells structured this brief sharing session stimulated the children to stretch their thinking.

Step 5: Cleanup and care of materials

The fifth graders will need less introduction and modeling. They've learned how to clean up other materials, and most of the children are quick to generalize these procedures and expectations to new materials.

"*It's time to clean up and get ready for math,*" *Ms. Wells says.* "*Now that you have practiced using the markers they will be out on the shelves so that you can get them whenever you need to use them. Take a moment to think about what you will need to do to get the markers back in their storage place so that they are in good shape for the next time someone wants to use them." She pauses. "Now go clean up."*

As the children put away the markers, Ms. Wells says, "You are really getting this done efficiently."

Noticing that the children at one table are preparing to carry their container of markers to the shelves while some markers lie on the floor beneath the table, she says to them, "Stop. What are you forgetting?"

The children look at each other uncertainly, and then they look back at the table. "Oh, there're more markers on the floor!" one says hitting his head in mock consternation. He and another student reach down to pick them up while their tablemates wait.

Once all the students are again seated at their tables, Ms. Wells begins the math lesson.

Guided Discovery

Although the students were familiar with cleanup routines, Ms. Wells took the time to observe carefully, reinforce appropriate behavior, and quickly redirect students as needed. If this group had been less adept with cleanup routines,

Ms. Wells would have asked one or two children to model just as Ms. Martell did with the younger children. Careful modeling and practice of transitions and cleanup is just as important in the upper elementary grades as it is in the primary grades, and for some groups these procedures may need more modeling and practice than for others. Teachers will need to use their judgment about how much modeling their particular group needs in order to be successful. If in doubt, take time to have children model!

**Chapter
Two**

FINE TUNINGS

Q. *When in the school year can I use Guided Discoveries?*

A. Guided Discoveries can happen at any point in the year but are used most extensively at the beginning of the year when children are becoming acquainted with basic classroom materials and routines. In addition to introducing materials, teachers might use Guided Discovery to introduce children to independent use of classroom libraries, or even school libraries, writing centers, or playground equipment.

Fine Tunings

Later in the school year, teachers can use Guided Discoveries from time to time to introduce materials being brought into use for the first time, or to expand and develop children's use of materials that they have used before in teacher-prescribed ways. For example, I often teach my students to use graph paper to make bar graphs early in the school year. Later, I may use a Guided Discovery of graph paper before offering it as a material for Academic Choice lessons in spelling and mathematics.

Q. *Do I always do Guided Discovery with the whole class?*

A. In this chapter's examples, the teachers did Guided Discoveries with the whole class. But Guided Discoveries may be conducted with small groups while other students work independently. Small-group Guided Discoveries work especially well when there are not enough materials for the entire class to use at once, or with complex or messy materials that require more teacher oversight before children are ready to work with them independently. I usually introduce materials such as watercolors and modeling clay in small groups.

Q. *Can I do Guided Discovery for any classroom material?*

A. Some classroom supplies are not appropriate for Guided Discoveries because there is only one way (or perhaps two or three ways) to use them appropriately. Teachers should use modeling and practice to introduce materials such as games, puzzles, some computer software, basic procedures for using computers, and worksheets. However, Guided Discovery is a great way to introduce many classroom supplies, including:

pencils	pens	colored pencils
scissors	staplers	crayons
tape	textbooks	dictionaries
globes	hole punches	glue
construction paper	libraries	maps
clay	encyclopedias	paints
math manipulatives	blocks	graph paper
rulers	protractors	Legos
some computer applications and software		dice

PART TWO

PLANNING, WORKING, REFLECTING
ACADEMIC CHOICE STEP-BY-STEP

As students begin to gain experience and comfort with making choices in school, with routines and behaviors that support independent action, and with some basic classroom tools and materials, they are ready to begin full-fledged Academic Choice lessons. To deepen understanding of how Academic Choice functions in the daily life of the classroom, Part Two gives a closer look at the three phases of Academic Choice: planning, working, and reflecting.

The importance of planning, working, and reflecting

The act of making a choice does not lead to increased learning on its own. Children need certain structures to assure that they will grow from the experience of choosing how or what to learn. As discussed in the introduction, planning, working, and reflecting is an optimal sequence for learning. For this reason, Academic Choice projects always consist of these three distinct phases.

After teachers introduce choice activities, students engage in planning what they will do. This encourages them to initiate active involvement in the lesson by making a reasoned decision and considering what they will need in order to act on their decision. Once students have made a plan and the teacher has approved the plan, students move into the working phase. During the working phase, both teachers and students engage in behaviors that produce a cycle of exploration and feedback leading to increasingly skillful and thoughtful student products. When work stops, reflecting begins. Children must look back upon their actions and products to examine what they have and have not accomplished before they can fully assimilate new knowledge and make it their own. Reflection inevitably leads back to planning when insights influence how a child goes about planning for his or her next choice activity.

Scheduling the three phases

These three phases of planning, working, and reflecting might all occur during the same session for simple Academic Choice lessons such as a practice session for spelling words. If there are forty-five minutes for the lesson, I could plan on taking about ten minutes for the introduction and planning phase, twenty-five minutes for the working phase including transitions, and ten minutes for the reflecting phase. If I have only thirty minutes for spelling, I might introduce the choices when I wrap up the spelling lesson of the previous day and post a sign-up chart where students can place their name beneath their choices as they enter the room the morning of the Academic Choice lesson. Then, when it is time for spelling, they can go right to work on their choices and still have time for a period of reflection at the end. Another alternative would be to schedule reflection for later in the day or have a few children present and reflect upon their spelling work at another time, such as during Morning Meeting. If I have only twenty minutes for spelling, the planning, working, and reflecting phases might each occur at a different time.

When Academic Choice projects extend over multiple class periods, the introduction and planning session could easily take one day's session. Children would work on the projects for several days, then take a day or sometimes two to present their work and write individual reflections about it.

Sue Majka used this format when she had the fourth grade students choose a science concept to teach to the rest of the class. The first day, they worked in groups to create a written plan for teaching the concept. After Sue had checked and agreed to the plans, they spent several days preparing their lessons. Each group taught the lesson they had prepared and took questions. As part of the reflecting phase, students recorded something they had learned from each group's presentation and something they liked about it. Each group could then use this feedback to help them reflect on the success of their work.

Structuring and facilitating Academic Choice lessons

Part Two is divided into three chapters, one each for the three phases of Academic Choice: planning, working, and reflecting. In each chapter, you'll find information about structuring and facilitating that phase and an example of the phase in action accompanied by my discussion of the teacher's decisions.

Part Two

Word Work —

sign up chart for place they want to be

Goal: Show what you have
learned about the geography
of your country using your
research tools.

Puppet Show/Quiz Show   Clay
1. Jon   1. ~~Apoosa~~ Arlen
2. megan   2. Hope
3. Lauren   3. ~~Fritzeb~~ Elizabeth
4. Mckee   4. Maggie

Paper and Art Supplies   Writing
1.   1.
2.   2.
3.   3.
4.   4.

Blocks - Pattern, Unifix, Legos   Make a game
1. Joshua   1. Alo
2. Aaliyah   2.
3.   3.
4. Nick   4.

Chapter Three

PLANNING PHASE
OF ACADEMIC CHOICE

I n a first grade classroom, students sit in a circle on the meeting rug. Their teacher has presented them with a list of three choices of how to practice counting by 2s. After giving them a moment to consider the three choices, she says, "Now turn to your neighbor and talk about which choice you'd like and why." Children eagerly begin conversations. After a minute, the teacher rings a chime and children stop their conversations and look at her. "OK," she says, "Let's go around the room and each of you say what you're going to do."

Down the hall in a third grade classroom, the students also sit in a circle on the meeting rug. The teacher stands next to a whiteboard where he's listed four choices for an Academic Choice research project that will help the students learn about town history. The choices include Internet research, interviewing older community members, going to the library to read back issues of the town paper, and reading a variety of town history books. Interviewing people and going to the town library will require more attention from the teacher, so he limits the number of students who make these choices by drawing six lines below the two choices. He's just finished explaining each of the choices. "I'd like you to think for a minute about a first and second choice. Since there are limited sign-up spaces for two of these choices, you might not get your first choice. When you've got a first and second choice in mind, put your thumb up." When he sees all the thumbs up, he says, "I'm going to call on you in alphabetical order, but I'm going to start with the letter m so that means Jason Moriarty gets to choose first."

In the sixth grade classroom upstairs, students sit at their worktables filling in a written work plan. They're about to embark on a unit-long Academic Choice as part of their study of marine biology. They get to choose an animal to research and a way to show what they've learned. The day before, their teacher explained all the choices, and they had a

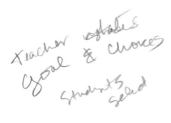

group discussion about what would be involved in each choice. The choices include making a diorama with captions, writing a report, or creating a picture book. The children had an opportunity to talk with a partner about pros and cons of various choices and then brought those ideas back to the larger group. Today they'll fill out draft planning sheets, which they'll show their teacher. She might have some suggestions or questions that they'll consider, then students will write a final plan for the teacher to approve. Once everyone has gotten a plan approved, the children will gather in a circle, and individuals will have an opportunity to share their plans out loud, if they'd like.

The planning phase is the first step in any Academic Choice lesson. This phase consists of two parts. First, teachers introduce the goal of the lesson and the choices that are available, then students make and commit to choices.

Planning Phase of Academic Choice

In simple Academic Choice projects, children might verbally name a choice or sign their name on a choice board. For more complex projects, children might complete a written planning sheet that outlines how they will enact their choice. In either case, the teacher provides a structure that helps children think through their decisions. With repeated opportunities to choose and plan their work, children develop the capacity to think ahead, visualize potential outcomes, consider what will be required to make those outcomes real, and make judgments about how effectively the chosen activities and materials will meet the goals of the lesson.

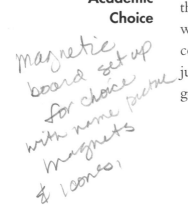

Time frame

The time required for the planning phase ranges from five minutes to one class session depending on the complexity of the choice activities and the length of the entire Academic Choice project.

Introducing the choices

Careful introduction of the choices helps children make good decisions based on an understanding of the lesson's goals and an awareness of skills and materials required to complete each choice.

Introducing Choices

When introducing the choices, teachers will want to:

1. **Put the choices into a context**

2. **Make sure the children understand all the options**

3. **Decide whether to present concrete examples of possible products**

Put the choices into a context

Before introducing specific choices, teachers need to present the context of those choices. What is the content of the lesson? What are the goals? This can be a brief statement ("Today we are going to practice spelling words from our list"), but it's important that children understand what they are doing and why they are doing it so that they can begin to connect making a choice and reaching a stated goal ("I will practice my spelling list by making a word-find puzzle").

Make sure the children understand all the options

Next, the teacher presents the available choices, making sure that all the students fully understand the options. There are several ways to present the choices. When choices are few and simple, you might just give them orally. But for more complicated choices or a longer list of choices, you'll want to write a list on a board or chart. At times, you'll want to display options. For example, to arouse interest in books that children might choose from during a reading lesson, you could hold up each book and flip through the pages. Or if choices involve games, such as math games, it would be helpful to display the games rather than try to describe them.

Decide whether to present concrete examples of possible products

**Planning
Phase of
Academic
Choice**

No matter how you initially present the choices, you'll need to decide whether or not to present concrete examples of products that could result from different options. If one of the choices is an activity that is fairly new to children, a concrete example might help them think about ways to use the activity in this particular setting. For example, a third grade teacher had just introduced letter-writing formats. When she planned an Academic Choice lesson to demonstrate how to understand the characters in a story, one of the choices was to write a letter from the point of view of one of the characters. To help students really understand how to use this skill in a new context, she created a sample letter to read to the children. If students have a great deal of experience with an option, concrete examples may not be necessary, although seeing concrete examples stimulates children's memories of how to do the various activities and gives them ideas for using the activities during Academic Choice.

Formats for student planning

The type of planning format teachers decide to have students use depends on the nature of the Academic Choice activities and, sometimes, the ages and past experiences of the children. With a little information and experience, teachers can make confident decisions about which planning format to use for any given Academic Choice lesson.

Student Planning Formats

**Student planning for Academic Choice
may occur in one of three ways:**

1. Oral planning

2. Sign-up charts and planning boards

3. Written planning sheets

Oral planning

This is the simplest form of planning and is most appropriate for very simple choices lasting for only one work period or less. For example, students can choose among three mathematics games for multiplication practice. They think about their choice and then tell the teacher. Teachers can keep notes on the choices children make to remind themselves and the children of their plans as needed.

The key is that children state their intention before enacting their choice. This simple act raises awareness and thoughtfulness about the act of deciding. It also gives teachers information that can help them guide and instruct students during the lesson.

One of the advantages of this type of planning is that it takes very little time, which is important in brief Academic Choice lessons, no matter how experienced the students are at planning. It also requires that students make a public commitment to a decision. This facilitates future reflection on whether the decision was a good one and why (or why not) and promotes growth in decision-making skills. For children with very little experience in planning, oral planning offers the possibility of success with making choices and provides a foundation for more complex planning.

Chapter Three

Sign-up charts and planning boards

Teachers provide a list of available options by displaying the written names of choice activities, by graphically representing the choices, or both. Beneath each choice, the teacher draws lines on which the teacher or the children can write the names of those who select that option.

In K–1 classrooms, teachers often use planning boards, which are relatively permanent classroom fixtures made out of bulletin boards, painted plywood, cloth covered homosote, heavy cardboard, or laminated poster board. Teachers write the choices on cards that they can easily attach or detach. Children place nametags beneath their chosen activity and remove the nametags when they finish the activity. You can find more information about how to create planning boards in *Classroom Spaces That Work* by Marlynn Clayton (Clayton 2001).

Teachers can create sign-up charts by listing available options on chart paper or a black or whiteboard and leaving space beneath each option for students' names. Unlike planning boards, sign-up charts are temporary, created for a specific lesson.

Planning Phase of Academic Choice

Sometimes, it's necessary to limit the number of children who can sign up for each option. There might be limited supplies, limited space, or concerns about noise. Sign-up charts work well to communicate which choices are limited and whether they still have openings. I draw lines beneath each option to indicate where students may sign their names. When the lines beneath an option are full, that option is closed. It is important to combine options that limit the number of students who can do them with at least two other options that are unlimited to assure that all students, even those who choose last, have a genuine choice.

To keep sign-up from being a free-for-all, teachers will want to call on students to come up to the board singly or in pairs. It's important to vary the order in which students choose so that the same children don't always get the first—or the last—choice. Students could pull numbered strips of paper out of a hat, or teachers could call on students in reverse alphabetical order or according to their birth dates or their heights. And teachers can ask students for creative ideas for varying the order. To save time, teachers might also write student names on a sign-up chart once each student has announced a choice.

Planning boards and sign-up charts serve as both teaching and management tools. They provide a public record of what the choices are, what choices children have made, what choices are open and closed, and who is choosing to do what. Such records provide children with more cues for their decision-making process and provide both teachers and children with prominent reminders of who can be expected to be where doing what.

Written planning sheets

For more open-ended choice activities or for projects that will continue for more than one class session, written planning sheets provide important support. Writing down a plan of action and listing necessary materials helps students assess whether they can realistically put their ideas into action. Written plans also provide a focus for discussion between teachers and students. Referring to the written plan might help students articulate their ideas; teachers can look at the plan and guide

Sample Student Planning Sheet, Grades 4–6, Research Project

Content area:

Topic:

Investigation:

Research sources:

Resources/work required:

Deadline:

Name: Date:

Co-workers (if any):

Teacher approval:

students toward adjustments that might be more realistic. Once the plans are completed and the teacher approves them, they serve as a guide to help students measure progress and stay on track.

There is not one correct way to make a student planning sheet; the format can address whatever areas the teacher thinks will help the students make good decisions. Planning sheets always include a place for students to write the general topic or procedure that they are choosing. Often there's a space to write what resources students will need or, when appropriate, where they will work and with whom they will work. For more complex activities, a planning sheet may provide space for students to write or draw ideas about what their finished products will look like or what information they will include.

Although planning sheets take more time for students to complete than sign-up charts or planning boards, they are an invaluable resource for students and teachers, particularly during longer projects. For example, Kristen Kugelman, a fourth grade teacher, assigned each of her students one of six geographic features they had studied in class. The students could choose to make a model of the feature, create a diorama, make a poster, or write a poem that expressed important elements of the feature.

Because students could make models and dioramas out of a wide variety of possible materials and the projects would take several days to complete, Kristen had each student complete a planning sheet before beginning the project. The planning sheet guided them to think through what they would do and what materials they would need in advance as well as what they would do to get more information about their landforms. The high quality of the students' work reflected the thought that went into the planning.

In the remainder of this chapter, you will get a glimpse of the planning phase in action in a third grade classroom, where the teacher, Mr. Kenyon, uses Academic Choice to structure a spelling lesson. Throughout the example, I pause and comment on what Mr. Kenyon is doing.

Planning Phase of Academic Choice

In Mr. Kenyon's classroom: the planning phase

Introducing the lesson's goals and the choices

Mr. Kenyon waits while the third graders settle into a circle in the meeting area. Once they are quiet, he says, "Today we're going to do an Academic Choice to practice spelling. The goal is to get better at spelling the words you missed on the pretest. There are a total of fifteen words on your weekly list, but you only need to practice the words that you misspelled. You will have a choice about how you practice. I've listed the choices here."

He points to the whiteboard and reads the four choices: make a word-find puzzle with graph paper; use cut-and-paste letters from magazines to spell the words; draw; or write. He explains each choice.

"You can make a word-find puzzle with graph paper," he says. "Remember when we did that for our practice before? What are some things you will need to think about if you choose to do this?"

A few hands go up, and Mr. Kenyon calls on the volunteers. They talk about needing to use the correct size graph paper, putting just one letter in each square, and using a pencil.

"All good points," responds Mr. Kenyon. "I have an example here. This is a word-find puzzle that Ally did last week." He holds it up so that all can see and highlights its strengths: she filled every space, wrote the words neatly below the puzzle, and used each word twice. "Using each word twice makes it more interesting," he says, "and it gave her more practice spelling the words." He posts Ally's puzzle on the whiteboard for future reference.

Mr. Kenyon points to the second choice, cutting and pasting letters from magazines. "Here's how I practiced some of the words with cutting and pasting," he says. He holds up a sheet of construction paper with three of the spelling words spelled out of letters cut from magazines and glued onto the paper. "I even found a picture of this word raincoat *and put it next to the word." He notes that it took a while to get all the words spelled this way. He gives them a hint about a good way to proceed: "I started by finding the letters for the words that were hardest to spell to make sure I got practice with them. I'll put this example on the board too." He attaches it next to the word-find puzzle.*

As he points to the third choice, drawing, he pretends to be puzzled. "How could you use drawing to practice spelling? Remember the goal is to practice spelling the words that are hard for you."

"You could write the word so that it makes a kind of picture. Like raincoat *could be written in the shape of a raincoat."*

"You could make the letters fancy and colorful."

"You could make a border like a frame around the words after you write them."

"Those are some great ideas," Mr. Kenyon tells the group. "Another idea is to decorate the parts of the words that show a spelling pattern. Or you could color all the long vowels the same and all the silent vowels the same."

Mr. Kenyon points at the last choice. "Some people find that they learn to spell words the best when they just write them over and over," he says. "And sometimes people just feel like sitting and writing. So if you choose to write, you might copy the words over and over or you might write them in sentences or a short story."

Mr. Kenyon now points to a chart posted nearby:

Criteria for Good Work

- *Neat*

- *Complete*

- *Accurate*

"Take a minute to remember our criteria for good work. What other criteria for good work might you have for your spelling practice?"

The children suggest using the words more than once, creativity and originality, and concentrating on their work.

Planning Phase of Academic Choice

The spelling curriculum that Mr. Kenyon uses provides a list of fifteen words each week. Children take a pretest on Monday and perform various types of word sorts to reinforce patterns on Tuesday. On Wednesday and Thursday, they practice spelling the words on the list before taking the post-test on Friday.

Mr. Kenyon designed choices that would appeal to children with a range of learning styles and interests. Making word-find puzzles builds on spatial perception and mathematical thinking, the drawing option on visual arts. Writing draws on verbal skills, and cutting and pasting on kinesthetic skills. Additionally, as the students become more and more comfortable with the social and academic climate in their classroom, this range of options offers opportunities to take risks and develop skills in areas that are not strengths.

Mr. Kenyon also designed options that used familiar techniques. They all had experience creating word-find puzzles and writing spelling words in a list or sentences. And they had general experience with cutting and pasting and with drawing, although they had not applied these techniques to spelling practice.

He decided to give examples of word-find puzzles and cut-and-paste practice sheets. Giving the example of cutting and pasting as it applied to spelling practice gave the children all the additional information they needed to make an informed decision about whether or not to choose this option. It took Mr. Kenyon about fifteen minutes to prepare the example. Doing this helped him make sure that this option would work—and he had fun!

Mr. Kenyon decided he did not need to show his class an example of drawing the spelling words because drawing was very familiar to them even though they'd never applied it to spelling. The children had a great deal of experience and a broad repertoire of ideas for drawing with markers and colored pencils at this point in the year. He felt that an example was not only unnecessary but might inhibit the children's own creativity.

Since writing spelling words was also a familiar task, he decided not to give an example of that as well. However, only one student selected writing. It may be that more students will select writing the next time similar choices are offered. It may be that when the boy who selected writing shares his work during the reflecting phase of the lesson, more students will become inspired to try this as a way to practice spelling. But if this doesn't happen, Mr. Kenyon might want to provide an engaging example of using writing to practice during a subsequent introduction to an Academic Choice for spelling practice. This might generate more interest in it.

Student planning

"Those are the choices. Take a minute and think quietly to yourself about what you would like to do today." He pauses while the children think. After a moment, he says, "Now turn to your neighbor and take turns telling each other what choices you are thinking about and why."

A babble of voices rises as students talk to each other. Two girls share ideas for using drawing to practice the words; a boy tells his neighbor that he just feels like writing the words today. He is tired, he says.

When the children have talked for about three minutes, the teacher gives a signal for attention, waits for silence, and then says, "Raise your hand if you choose to make word-find puzzles today."

Six students raise hands and Mr. Kenyon writes their names on the whiteboard beneath this option. He goes through the rest of the options in the same way. Only one student, the boy he overheard earlier, chooses writing. Ten have chosen to draw, and five have chosen to cut and paste.

Mr. Kenyon first gives children a moment to digest the information about the choices and perhaps consider more than one before making a final decision. Earlier in the year he had modeled this process with a think-aloud strategy. If he had not done so in the past, or if he had thought that some of his students could use a review, he could have modeled decision making for them before he instructed them to think about the options.

Mr. Kenyon decided to have the children talk to each other about their plans before committing themselves. This is another strategy that supports growth in the decision-making process. Children, especially younger ones, think by speaking. By giving them a chance to talk about what they were choosing and why, Mr. Kenyon helped them put more thought into their plan.

Now, with thoughtful plans in place, the children are ready to move into the working phase of Academic Choice.

Fine Tunings

FINE TUNINGS

Q. *There's a student in my class who just can't seem to settle on a choice. He is still musing over the options when the rest of the class is already at work.*

A. For some children, making choices can seem more like a burden than an opportunity. These students need to begin with more structure and fewer options than their classmates. Try limiting this student to two options for a while. If he still has trouble deciding, agree on some arbitrary way of resolving the dilemma such as writing the choices on slips of paper and drawing one out of a hat. It might also be helpful to observe the child and perhaps have a discussion with him to see if you can figure out why making a decision is so difficult for him so that you can make appropriate adjustments to the selection process.

Chapter Three

Q. *My students sometimes want to change their choice after they have already begun an activity.*

A. Your response to this behavior will depend on the child and the situation. If the same children repeatedly ask to change activities, they probably need to learn persistence. In that case, I would require that they complete any activity they plan to do before changing to another one. Let students know this will be the expectation before they plan. Following a commitment through to completion, even if it turns out not to be the best choice, is a valuable learning experience. Over time, children make better and better decisions for themselves.

If children only ask to change activities occasionally, I check on their progress and discuss their reasons for wanting to change. Sometimes I can help them feel better about staying with their original choice. Sometimes making a change makes sense.

Q. *Whenever I have activities that involve writing as one of several choices, no one chooses to write.*

A. Writing is generally required of children several times a day in school. When they have a choice, they may want to do something else! You could try bringing more Academic Choice into writing lessons to increase students' engagement with writing. Perhaps they could choose genres or topics more frequently. You could also use forms of expression other than writing for some non–Academic Choice lessons to bring more balance into daily activities. Children could draw characters using descriptors in a book, for example, rather than writing a paragraph about them. Over time, they might find that they want to write.

Q. *I have a group of children who always choose whatever option the most popular girl in the class chooses.*

Fine Tunings

A. Sometimes making choices based on what friends are doing offers a good starting point for children who have little experience making independent choices. They think, "If the teacher won't tell me what to do, then I'll let another student let me know what to do!" Continue using the strategies described for building a strong foundation for Academic Choice, and focus especially on creating a safe, inclusive sense of community. Find ways to introduce activities that call upon a wide variety of strengths and learning styles so that each child can become known for strengths and leadership in some area. If need be, you can limit the number of children who can choose any one activity to encourage some children to make decisions on their own and try different things. You can also call on students to state their choice one at a time. Call on the leaders after many other children have made their selections.

Q. *I'm uncomfortable with teachers making their own examples of choice activities to show the children when they introduce the activities. Won't that discourage some children who will feel they can never make something as nice as the teacher's? It also seems like a lot of work for the teacher.*

A. You don't need an example of an activity every time you introduce an Academic Choice lesson. You'll only need examples when an activity is new to the children, few have chosen it in past sessions, or you are dissatisfied with the quality of the children's work on the activity. I have seen children take the examples as starting points and create wonderful pieces of work.

If you have a good example of a child's work, then use it. Otherwise, the only way to provide an example is to make it yourself. A teacher-made example should model only the beginning or the outline of a complete project and should only take you five or ten minutes to make. While it should not be sloppy, it certainly will not represent your best work! Make your example show work that is appropriate to the age group you teach.

Q. *Why didn't Mr. Kenyon ask the children for their ideas about different ways they could choose to practice their spelling?*

A. Until they have some basic knowledge and experience with at least a small range of different types of activities and with a somewhat larger range of tools and materials, many children have a hard time generating ideas that are both engaging and realistic. Thinking of activities that will achieve a particular learning goal might also be difficult for children who are inexperienced with Academic Choice. It can be a challenge for teachers! If teachers ask children to generate the activities before they are ready, Academic Choice lessons may become chaotic and frustrating, and learning goals are often lost in the confusion.

Once children are familiar with a variety of materials and activities and are comfortable with Academic Choice, they might be ready to brainstorm ideas for choices. This can lead to very rich Academic Choice lessons. Mr. Kenyon might introduce two options that he knows will be within the abilities of every child in the class and then ask, "What are some other ways you might choose to use classroom supplies to practice your spelling words?" As the children brainstorm, he could record their ideas, then select a few (or all) to add to the list of options.

Chapter Three

Work Cited

Clayton, Marlynn with Mary Beth Forton. 2001. *Classroom Spaces That Work*. Greenfield, MA: Northeast Foundation for Children (NEFC).

Chapter Four

WORKING PHASE
OF ACADEMIC CHOICE

I t's the third day of a multiday Academic *Choice project. The fourth graders have been studying trees. The goal was for them to learn ten facts about trees. They each got to choose which tree they wanted to study and how to demonstrate what they've learned. In previous days, they wrote up their plans, the teacher approved them, and they did their research. Today they'll begin their work on a way to demonstrate their learning. At the beginning of the session, the teacher asks all the children to gather in the meeting area. She uses the time to check in with each student about what the student is going to do today and to answer any questions. Several students are making dioramas, but despite a reminder from the teacher about bringing in boxes from home, many have forgotten to do so. "How can you begin your project without boxes?" the teacher asks. The students decide they can sketch ideas and maybe begin cutting out figures for the boxes. After a few minutes, she dismisses the students to begin their work. Most students are working individually; a few are working in pairs. There's a low hum of excitement as they gather needed materials and settle at their worktables. The teacher observes them for a few minutes then begins to circulate around the room, pausing frequently to talk with students.*

During the working phase, children carry out their plans. In the process, they discover what strategies work and don't work, make needed adjustments to their plans, solve problems, make discoveries, and practice skills. Teachers observe, support students' efforts, and help them solve problems and extend their thinking. In addition to students having an opportunity to strengthen and consolidate new skills and learning, teachers and students both learn about students' learning styles and interests.

**Working
Phase of
Academic
Choice**

Time frame

The working phase begins when students have made a plan that the teacher approves. The time required for the working phase ranges from approximately twenty-five minutes to several class sessions depending on the complexity of the Academic Choice project.

Ensure a smooth transition from the planning phase

A smooth transition from planning to working establishes a calm, focused atmosphere, ideal for independent work. This transition is more likely to go smoothly if children are comfortable with routines such as moving from the meeting area to the working area, are familiar with materials they'll use, and are confident about the choices they made. This means that teachers need to take time to model and practice routines as needed throughout the year (see Chapter One), do Guided Discoveries of materials before setting up the Academic Choice experience (see Chapter Two), provide a clear explanation of choices, and coach children through the decision-making process (see Chapter One and Three).

During the transition, teachers should observe what children are doing. If one or two students are having difficulty gathering materials or settling to work, the teacher can redirect them. If many students are having difficulty, the teacher will want to stop the transition and address the problem area with further modeling and practice.

Begin with students working alone

When children are new to Academic Choice, I find it best to have them plan and work as individuals. This doesn't mean they're isolated as they work—children are free to interact with each other or not. In fact, the spontaneous interactions that often happen when children are engaged in their work can contribute to a lively, supportive learning community. But in these casual interactions, there's no pressure to reach agreement or share tasks. If negative interactions occur, it's easy to intervene and stop them since the success of the lesson does not hinge on children's working together.

Introduce partner or group work slowly

Once students have experience with Academic Choice as individuals and have practice with collaborative work skills (see Chapter One), I may start to assign children to pairs for some Academic Choice activities. Once the pairs can work together successfully, I may decide to assign students to small groups for some projects.

I only allow students to choose partners or groups for themselves if they have first been successful at working in teacher-assigned teams and if I feel confident that such self-determined groups will not cultivate cliques. Cliques can create a sense of threat and exclusion that undermines children's ability to think independently and learn well.

Pay attention to the teacher's role

While the children work independently on their chosen task, the teacher's job is to observe, support, and coach, sometimes working with the entire class and other times with individual students.

Teacher's Role While Children Are Working

The teacher's role during the working phase is like a dance. With experience, you'll find your own rhythm for:

1. **Stepping back to observe, facilitate, and encourage**

2. **Stepping in to coach as needed**

Stepping back to observe, facilitate, and encourage

Observing students during the working phase provides invaluable information about their evolving abilities, understandings, interests, and social involvements. Teachers can see whether children follow through on their plans and assess what gets in the way of successful completion. Noting who is dawdling, who has trouble getting started, who is sidetracked by a neighbor's conversation, who seems isolated as well as who is working well will guide individual interventions.

Careful observation also affords opportunities for giving good feedback to the whole group. By using encouraging and empowering language, teachers can reassure students and help them maintain focus. For example, a teacher could reinforce students' positive efforts at getting started with their work by saying, "I see everyone is gathering the supplies they need and moving calmly to their desks." If some children are getting caught up in loud conversations rather than starting their work, the teacher might say, "Remind me what it looks and sounds like when we're all working productively." And if one or several children persist in distracting behavior, the teacher could redirect them by saying something like, "Rose, you and Gianni need to sit separately."

Stepping in to coach as needed

As you observe, you'll notice who is eager to go and who is having a hard time getting started; who seems frustrated and who seems to be enjoying their work; who is struggling with remembering simple instructions and who is helping others remember what needs to be done. Coach as needed based on observations.

Working Phase of Academic Choice

Praise vs. Encouragement

One particular issue that comes up during Academic Choice is whether to use the language of praise or encouragement when responding to children's work. I prefer to encourage children by noticing and describing their good work rather than praise them with general terms like "Good job!"

In Academic Choice, the focus should be on the process of planning, working, and reflecting on work. Praise, however, often focuses more on the product than the process. Praise can also put pressure on children, leaving them with a sense that they need to live up to a goal of perfection. And finally, praise can make children dependent on the judgment of others, which can get in the way of children's ability to reflect on their own work.

Encouragement on the other hand focuses on the process. When I offer encouragement, I'm acknowledging children's ability to work toward their own goals and to define their own limits. And I give them specific and useful information about the work that they're doing.

This doesn't mean I never praise children. But praise is most effective when it's combined with something specific and descriptive about children's actions or work.

**Chapter
Four**

Ask open-ended questions

When a student needs some guidance, think about how to intervene in a way that allows the student to direct the work but also move toward success. For example, ask open-ended questions: "What do you want to do next?" or "You've cut out two words and there are ten minutes left. How will you finish the task?" or "What are your thoughts about . . . ?" Asking genuine questions can be a powerful strategy because teachers can learn a great deal about students' perspectives, which can help teachers support students' learning more effectively.

Before asking a question, you need to be sure it's an honest question rather than an indirect way to give advice or pass judgment. A teacher might ask, "Do you think that writing each word five times will be enough?" when he really means, "Writing each word five times won't help you meet the goal." When teachers ask rhetorical questions, they expect the student to give a predetermined answer. Though teachers often use rhetorical questions with the intention of softening a redirection, this strategy undermines the trust children need to have in their teachers. They are left to try to guess the "right" answer and risk being "wrong." It is far better to simply state the intended point.

Practice "perspective taking"

Sometimes the best intervention is to pause, look at the situation from the student's point of view, and then convey your understanding of why the student is approaching his work in a particular way: "Eddie, you're cutting out all the pictures you might need for your collage before putting anything on the paper. You'll have a lot of pictures to choose from." This technique is called "perspective taking" and is one of the most powerful approaches a teacher can use to support children's growth in autonomy, internal motivation, and personal responsibility. (Reeve 2002)

Working Phase of Academic Choice

Ask before offering direction

Once you've thought about the situation from the student's point of view, you might have ideas about how to proceed with the work. Again, pause and then

ask the student if they'd like to hear your suggestions. They might say "Sure!" but they might also say, "No thanks, I want to work this out on my own." That's okay! An honest question ("Would you like some help with this?") deserves an honest answer. If a student does not share a teacher's perception that there is a problem with her approach, or if she wants to solve the problem without the teacher's help, it's best to let her work independently, checking in periodically to monitor her progress. The student will learn more by trying out her own ideas and then fixing what didn't work than she will by simply following her teacher's direction, as long as the task is appropriately challenging for her. If the task were too hard for her to complete with at least ninety percent independence, it would not be appropriate for an Academic Choice.

Provide brief instruction, if needed and wanted

You might also help students who need a particular skill or piece of information. For example, you might briefly show a student how to use a ruler to make straight lines if you saw that the child had a particular need for this skill. Or you might provide vocabulary. "You've made a trapezoid there! See how it has four sides? That makes it a trapezoid." Choice activities offer wonderful opportunities for brief instruction that is all the more powerful because it directly relates to students' self-initiated activity.

Check in with everybody at some point

It's also important to check in on those who appear to be cruising along on their own. Sometimes it may seem like an unrealistic luxury to have time to work with children who are doing fine on their own. But these students will also benefit from their teacher's attention as they work on their projects. Simple words of encouragement will help them stay focused and productive.

However, I know I have days when it seems all I can do is put out fires. If I find that this is happening regularly, however, I call a temporary moratorium on Academic Choice and re-examine what I need to do to assure that most students can work independently most of the time when they have choices. I may need to simplify the choice activities or offer better introductions. I may need to go back and redo or extend modeling and practice or Guided Discoveries in problem areas. I may need to reassess the lesson's content and procedures to make sure that the lesson is developmentally appropriate for the students who are having difficulty. When I determine and correct the problem, I return to Academic Choice as a regular strategy.

Help students practice time management

Since children are working independently, the working phase offers a great opportunity for them to practice time management skills. But you'll need to give them some structure and guidance. For example, in a one-session Academic Choice work period, I might give a five- or ten-minute warning that the period is almost over. Some children will be so engaged in their work that they'll find it hard to stop. In that case, I might remind them of other times when they can return to the work if they are not done. I'll also pay attention to the kinds of materials children are using: children who are using messier materials, such as cutting and pasting, might need an earlier warning than children using simpler materials.

Leah Carson, a first grade teacher, sets a large timekeeping device (TimeTimer™, see Appendix D) that students can see from anywhere in the classroom. If the work period is twenty minutes long, for example, she turns the hand on the timer to twenty, then it ticks off the minutes backward to zero. When I observed an Academic Choice lesson in Leah's classroom, the children checked in with the timer frequently. When Leah gave the five-minute warning, no one was taken by surprise.

In Mr. Kenyon's room—the working phase

Making the transition to working

Once all the children have made their choices, Mr. Kenyon dismisses them by table groups. As the small groups gather supplies and return to their tables, Mr. Kenyon watches and coaches.

"I notice that people are getting their supplies quickly. You are really getting good at independent work," he tells them.

Jason, a member of the last group to be dismissed, wanders over to watch a friend begin work before getting his own materials. "Jason, what do you need to be doing right now?" Mr. Kenyon asks.

"Getting my supplies," Jason responds and begins to do so.

Mr. Kenyon continues to observe the class from his vantage point on the meeting rug. He notices a group of children clumped around a shelf waiting to get containers of markers while the two in front go through several containers to pick the ones with the most colors of markers.

"Sara and Marcus, just take the containers nearest you so everyone can get going on their work. If you need a color, you can always borrow it from someone."

Working Phase of Academic Choice

This transition went smoothly. The children knew what supplies they needed because Mr. Kenyon provided examples of different activities. They were familiar with the relevant classroom supplies because they had explored the supplies in Guided Discoveries. Mr. Kenyon placed supplies where students could get them on their own and taught them procedures for doing so. And the students had lots of experience with getting started on independent work. This left Mr. Kenyon free to observe and coach his students, using reinforcing, reminding, and redirecting language:

- Mr. Kenyon was able to **reinforce** students' good efforts through statements such as "I notice that people are getting their supplies quickly."

- Noticing that Jason was talking to friends rather than getting ready to work, Mr. Kenyon offered a **reminder** that also empowered Jason to take responsibility for himself. "What do you need to be doing right now?" he asked.

- When he saw a backlog of students waiting to get markers, he was able to assess the nature of the problem immediately and offer a quick **redirection** to get things moving again.

Chapter Four

Teacher as coach

Once all the students are settled and ready to work, Mr. Kenyon begins to circulate among them. He goes first to Jason, who has a stack of four old magazines, a piece of construction paper, scissors, and glue before him. Jason quickly flips through one magazine, then another. Halfway through the second magazine, Jason stops at an advertisement for cars and cuts the page out of the magazine. Mr. Kenyon sees no sign of his spelling list. "What spelling word are you going to spell first?" he asks Jason.

Jason looks at him in surprise. "I just thought I'd cut out these letters and then when I have a bunch of them I can use them to spell the words."

"Well, that is one approach to this job. You get a lot of letters, then pick out the ones you need for the spelling words. Sounds like you have a plan in mind. I'll be interested to see how it works for you."

Working Phase of Academic Choice

Mr. Kenyon first checked in with Jason because he noticed that Jason might be having a hard time getting started on his work. Before intervening, however, Mr. Kenyon took a moment to watch Jason work. He learned that Jason was ready to focus on the cut-and-paste materials and that he had a plan.

Although Mr. Kenyon had some concerns about Jason's approach, he didn't offer any suggestions. Instead, he asked a question: "What spelling word are you going to spell first?" The question focused Jason on the learning objective for this particular lesson and simultaneously expressed faith in Jason's intentions and ability to figure out how to go about this task himself.

Jason's response to the question indicated that he did not share his teacher's approach to the task. In fact, he seemed more interested in cutting than spelling! Mr. Kenyon was concerned that Jason wouldn't have a chance to actually spell the words in the allotted time. But he was pleased that Jason had developed an original plan for completing the specified task at his own initiative and seemed invested in it.

Although practicing the spelling words was important, it wasn't the only goal Mr. Kenyon had for the students. He also wanted students to develop confidence as independent learners, as well as initiative, investment in learning, the ability to think critically, and the willingness to accept responsibility for their decisions. He was concerned that offering direction to Jason might have undermined the long-term goal of initiative and independence.

Mr. Kenyon knew that Jason had reasoned out a plan to which he was already committed. He was not open to another plan at this point. If Mr. Kenyon offered direction, Jason would have either complied or rebelled. In either case, he would have disengaged from the work and completed it, or not, with minimal care and thought. Not only would his investment have been undermined, but he would have also probably not learned any more spelling words than he would have by following his initial plan.

For this reason, Mr. Kenyon opted to restrain from offering advice. Another benefit of taking time to observe children as they work is that it gives teachers time to think these things through! "Sounds like you have a plan," he said.

Asking genuine questions

Mr. Kenyon next checks in with Chris, who has already written two of the spelling words five times each and is beginning to copy the third one. "You've already gotten a lot done, Chris!" Mr. Kenyon encourages him.

"Yeah, this is easy. That's why I picked it. I didn't feel like doing something that takes a long time." Chris continues to write as he speaks.

"Do you think that writing each word five times will be enough to remember how to spell them?"

"Yeah."

"Which words are the hardest for you?"

*"*Because* and* caught.*"*

"Yeah, those are hard words," Mr. Kenyon agrees. "You know at the rate you're working, you will probably finish copying all the words five times before the period is over. What could you do to get extra practice with those two words?"

Chris stops writing and thinks for a moment. "I could find someone else who's done and practice spelling those words over and over to them."

"Yes, that could work. What if no one is free to work with you?"

Chris doodles and thinks. "I could just turn my spelling list over and try to write the words without looking and then check and see if I got them right."

"Sounds like you've got two good options." Mr. Kenyon smiles at Chris and looks around the class once again.

When Mr. Kenyon asked Chris whether he thought writing each word five times would be enough to learn them, it was a genuine question. After a few weeks in Mr. Kenyon's class, Chris knew that his teacher really wanted to know what he thought so he answered honestly.

When Chris shared his opinion, Mr. Kenyon accepted it as information and moved to extend his student's thinking and sense of personal responsibility by asking him what he could do to get more practice with the two words he thought might be difficult for him. He guided his thinking with questions that focused Chris on important factors, but left him to make the final decision about what, if anything, he would do.

Giving feedback

Mr. Kenyon notices that Jason now has a small pile of letters cut out, but still no evidence of the spelling list. He has stopped cutting and is bragging to the other children at his table about a movie he saw last weekend.

Mr. Kenyon walks over to Jason and comments, "Jason, we have ten minutes left for spelling today. Looks like you have a lot to do." Jason turns to his letters and begins to arrange some of them into a word.

As Mr. Kenyon continues to observe the students' work, he sees some interesting designs emerging among the drawers. One student has drawn large block- printed letters spelling out each of four words. Each letter has been shaded in with a soft mixture of color created by crayons turned on their sides.

Mr. Kenyon also notices Tonya showing Nicky and James her drawing. She is a talented artist, but she's held herself apart from the other children until now. This is real progress, he thinks.

In another part of the room, Mr. Kenyon watches as two boys encase words, written in markers, inside geometric patterns created by tracing pattern blocks. Next to them Shayna experiments with adding leaves and flowers to each letter in a manner similar to illuminated letters.

"Now that's an idea I hadn't thought of!" Mr. Kenyon tells her. "How did you think of decorating the letters like that?"

Shayna ducks her head and grins shyly. "I just thought of it," she says.

"Well, keep on thinking, Shayna!"

Jason continues to talk about movies, but now he also cuts out more letters. Others who chose to cut and paste have glued letters for several words onto construction paper. Two, who sit side by side, inform each other of particular letters they seek and cut out let- ters for each other as well as themselves. They have already completed seven words each.

"I see so many good ideas!" Mr. Kenyon announces to the class. "Some of you are really into working on your own and some of you are helping each other out."

Mr. Kenyon provided reinforcing feedback by naming specific behaviors and products rather than by using general praise. Using phrases such as "I see many good ideas" and "I notice that some work alone and some help each other" gives children much more useful and empowering information than "Good job, everyone" or "This class is being respectful."

When Mr. Kenyon concentrated on interactions with individuals, he was able to build a warm relationship with quiet, self-sufficient Shayna as well as with distractible Jason, and foster growth that might not otherwise occur.

Perspective taking

He checks in with Latisha, who is flipping through the dictionary, her word-find puzzle on hold. She has neatly written each spelling word inside a square grid. The words are arranged vertically, horizontally, and diagonally. "Did you find what you needed in the dictionary, Latisha?"

"I'm just looking for some more words I can put in this puzzle. The spelling words don't fill it up enough."

"Oh, I see what you mean. You made a pretty big square. Finding a bunch of new words seems hard, though."

"Yeah, it's hard to decide which ones. I'm trying to find the ones that are short."

"Finding shorter words helps. Would you like to hear another idea, or do you really want to use the dictionary?"

"I'll hear another idea." Latisha looks at Mr. Kenyon hopefully.

"You could just use the spelling words again. I see you haven't put any words backward yet. If you start with the last letter and spell the word backward, that makes a challenging puzzle, and you don't have to look up more words."

"Oh, yeah, I like that!" Latisha beams.

This interaction with Latisha is an example of perspective taking. When Latisha explained why she was looking through the dictionary, he looked at things from her point of view and responded, "I see what you mean." Then, with Latisha's perspective as a starting point, he expanded a bit. "Finding a bunch of new words seems hard, though." He stopped with that observation and Latisha picked up on it and agreed.

Now they were sharing a common problem and working in concert. Even then, Mr. Kenyon asked her if she wanted advice before he gave it. This demonstrated respect for the child's perspective and her ability to solve her own problems. When Latisha indicated that she did want to hear her teacher's idea, she effectively took initiative and maintained control over how she went about her chosen task. Simultaneously, she opened her mind to new ideas. Mr. Kenyon facilitated all this positive energy in Latisha because he began by slowing down long enough to learn about and share her perspective, without forcing his perspective upon her.

Wrapping up

Mr. Kenyon continues to alternate general observation and feedback to the class with inter-actions with individual students. He gives a five-minute warning and advises those who are cutting and pasting to begin cleanup soon, then checks in one more time with Jason.

"How did your plan work out, Jason?" Mr. Kenyon sees that he has three spelling words glued to his construction paper and a large pile of cutout letters. He is, once again, flipping through a magazine.

"I got a ton of letters, but I didn't cut out enough a's. I've only done three words and I've used up all my a's, so I have to find more. I have lots more words to do."

"Oh, that's a problem. It's going to be hard to get all the rest of the words done in five minutes, isn't it?" Mr. Kenyon commiserates. "Would you like some ideas that might help?"

"No, I'll get it, don't worry, Mr. Kenyon. I kind of like finding the a's."

"What will you do to finish your work and practice all the spelling words? We've only got a couple more minutes."

Jason thinks and cuts. "Could I finish after math instead of going to music?"

"No, music is required. But finishing up later today is a good idea. When else could you do it?"

"I'll work on it whenever I get my other work done, and if I still have more I'll do it for homework."

"That will work. You can just show it to me when you're done. But if you want to get it done faster, let me know. I have some ideas."

"Okay." Jason bows over his scissors and cuts another letter.

"Time to bring your work to the meeting rug," Mr. Kenyon announces to the class.

Once Mr. Kenyon was sure that students were finishing up their work for the session, he checked in with Jason, who was not even close to completing his task. Once again, Mr. Kenyon began with a question rather than advice or a direction. He wanted to know what Jason was thinking before deciding how to respond to the situation. Mr. Kenyon reflected the boy's perspective, "It's going to be hard . . ." and then, as he did with Latisha, asked Jason if he would like some ideas. Unlike Latisha, Jason wanted to pursue his own plan, and he was comfortable telling his teacher so. He even offered Mr. Kenyon reassurance!

Mr. Kenyon wanted Jason to practice thinking for himself and solving his own problems. There was something about cutting out a lot of letters first and then spelling the words later that was important to Jason. Maybe it was impor-tant simply because it was his own plan, or maybe it revealed something about

(margin note:) **Working Phase of Academic Choice**

Jason's learning style and approach to problem solving in general. As Jason's teacher, Mr. Kenyon wanted to use this opportunity to learn more about Jason by observing his approach to this task.

Mr. Kenyon knew that he also needed to provide Jason with some limits, so he asked a question, "What will you do to finish your work and practice all the spelling words?" This question reminded Jason of the lesson's goal and let him know that he was accountable for the outcome of his experiment.

By figuring out for himself how to finish the work, Jason gained a sense of competence along with motivation to complete the work. Of course, if Jason showed that he was not able or willing to follow his plan, Mr. Kenyon would have stepped in with direction and, if need be, logical consequences. (See Brady et al., *Rules in School,* for a discussion of logical consequences.)

Mr. Kenyon's five-minute warning helped his students prepare to disengage. They were able to bring their work to a close and gather again in the meeting circle to reflect on their thinking and work.

**Chapter
Four**

FINE TUNINGS

Q. *What do you do when you have students who never seem to finish their choice activity?*

A. Take time to observe these students for a while to understand why they are not finishing. Some children become so engrossed in processes they lose sight of the goal of a task. This was true for Jason in Mr. Kenyon's class when he spent almost the entire work time cutting out letters rather than spelling words with them. It might help to break the task down into smaller goals that the student can reach more quickly. Mr. Kenyon could have given Jason two spelling words and told him to spell them with cutout letters before he checked in with him again.

Fine Tunings   You could also try the approach that Mr. Kenyon did. He attempted to trigger Jason's thinking about the problem through careful questioning and structured reflection. This is less efficient in the short term, but more effective over time.

It's also helpful to plan for other times during the day when students can complete their work. Sometimes, children simply need more time than the scheduled period allows. School schedules are very tight these days!

Q. *What do you do about children who finish their work before the period is over?*

A. I generally tell them to make another choice. You could also have them help others who have a lot left to do, or you could challenge them to go a step or two further with their first choice. I might say, "See if you can find three more facts about your topic," for example. They could also use the time to complete a written reflection about their work. Sometimes such reflections generate revisions or extensions of their work as well.

Q. *Children need to work independently for Academic Choice, but I have one or two who repeatedly ask me for help or feedback about their work.*

A. First, check to be sure that they've chosen appropriately challenging activities. If they've chosen an activity that they can't complete with relative independence, you'll need to make some adjustments. Check in with them before they begin work to help them plan what they will do and how they will do it. Unsolicited time with you in the beginning might go a long way toward alleviating anxiety and setting up a positive experience for them. Promise that you will check in every five minutes and do so. Set a timer that both you and the child can see, if possible. Challenge them to solve problems on their own or to wait for you between check-ins. Teach children what they can do to get help when you are not available and allow time to practice these strategies.

Works Cited

Brady, Kathryn, Mary Beth Forton, Deborah Porter, Chip Wood. 2003. *Rules in School*. Greenfield, MA: Northeast Foundation for Children (NEFC).

Reeve, Johnmarshall. 2002. "Self-Determination Theory Applied to Educational Settings." *Handbook of Self-Determination Research*. Edward Deci and Richard Ryan, eds. Rochester, NY: The University of Rochester Press.

Chapter Four

Chapter Five

REFLECTING PHASE
OF ACADEMIC CHOICE

irst graders have been reading the book Henry Climbs a Mountain. *(Johnson 2003) Their goal was to relate a theme of the book to their personal experience. They had a choice of how to show what they imagined: make a picture book, paint or draw a scene, make a cut-and-paste collage, write a story, or make a model using blocks or modeling clay. It's now time for reflecting. The teacher gathers them on the meeting rug. Three students will show their work to the group and respond to questions and comments, then each student will turn to a neighbor and together the partners will discuss the focus question: "What is your favorite part of your work and why?"*

Fifth graders have been learning how to order sets of fractions. Their goal for this Academic Choice lesson was to place sets of eight fractions, including halves, thirds, fourths, sixths, and twelfths, in order from least to greatest. They could choose among three ways to show and compare the fractions: fraction bars, pattern blocks, and drawing. As the working phase draws to a close, the teacher rings a chime to let students know it's time to wrap up their work and move into the reflecting phase. "As we finish today's lesson," she says, "I'd like you to take out your math journals. Find a fresh page and put today's date at the top. First, write down a description of what you did today. Then think about this question and write a brief response to it: 'What was one thing you learned about how to order fractions that you didn't know before?'" As she speaks, she points to the flip chart where she's written the question. There's a rustle of paper as students open their math journals and begin to write.

In the reflecting phase of Academic Choice, students look back on the process and content of their work. Reflecting is essential to the success of Academic Choice because it allows students to assimilate what they have learned: What in their work makes them uncomfortable or surprised or excited? How did their work change the way they think about a topic? How did their work reinforce previous ideas? Students also consider how their own actions influence the outcomes of their work: What helps them learn? What gets in the way of learning? And finally, they have a chance to self-evaluate: What have they done well? What didn't go well? Why?

Time frame

The reflecting phase usually begins when the working phase is complete, although in multiday Academic Choice lessons, students might benefit from a brief daily reflection on work in progress. The time required for the reflecting phase ranges from ten minutes to several work periods depending on the complexity of the Academic Choice project. Although it's best if the reflecting phase follows immediately after the working phase, the reflecting can happen later if time is tight.

Making the transition from working to reflecting

Many teachers have children go straight from their work to reflection, deferring cleanup. When children are engaged in their work, they might be reluctant to

Reflecting Phase of Academic Choice

stop for cleanup but willing to stop and talk about their work. Talking and thinking about their work can provide a sense of closure that makes it easier to disengage from their projects and focus on the details of cleanup. However, there's no hard and fast rule about this, and you'll need to discover what works best for the children in your classroom.

Kinds of reflecting

Reflecting can occur in several formats. Often, children gather in a group for a kind of reflecting that is called "representing" because it combines reflecting with presenting. At other times, children might fill out individual reflection sheets, which only the individual child and the teacher see. Sometimes, reflecting combines the public forum of representing with private time to fill out reflection sheets. Finally, reflecting can also include a format for self-evaluation.

Chapter Five

Kinds of Reflecting

1. **Representing**

2. **Individual reflecting**

3. **Self-evaluation**

Representing

This is the most common form of reflecting. Students might share either completed work or work in progress. In addition to showing the product of the work, students might discuss aspects of the work itself (the composition of a drawing, the characters in a story), their thoughts and opinions about that work ("I thought this drawing was successful because . . ."), or the processes undertaken for accomplishing the work ("I started out by . . ."), depending on their teacher's goal for a given representing meeting. Listeners interact with presenters in structured ways that further develop the thinking of both parties.

Representing meetings usually involve the whole class, particularly early in the year when students are learning the routines for presenting. Once students have learned how to make a clear presentation, respond well to focus questions,

Reflecting Phase of Academic Choice

listen thoughtfully, and formulate useful questions and comments, they can then do representing in small groups or with partners from time to time.

Representing gains much of its power from its basis in the principles of social constructivism, which state that the greatest cognitive growth occurs through social interaction. (Vygotsky 1978; Rogoff 1990) Representing deepens learning in several ways:

- Representing provides students with the kind of recognition that comes from genuine interactions. Recognition that says, for example, "I see what you mean" or "That's an interesting idea" helps students appreciate their own work as they see it reflected in the mirror of others' observations and questions.

- Representing encourages analytical thinking about both the products of the Academic Choice work and the process. For example, in addition to saying "I like the story I wrote" or "I don't like my drawing," children learn to think through and articulate why they feel as they do. What specifically do they like or not like? What do they wish they'd done differently? What felt good about the process? How did the process influence the outcome?

What would they do differently next time? The answers to questions such as these will help children produce higher quality work in the future.

- Representing exposes children to a range of ideas, which might inspire new directions in their own future work. I have found that when Academic Choice seems to be losing its spark and student work seems uninspired or of poor quality, a greater emphasis on representing often reinvigorates children's creativity and enthusiasm. Over time, the quality and variety of the work done during choice sessions improves, partly because of what children learn from each other.

In a representing meeting, the whole class gathers to share and discuss the work that happened during Academic Choice. Representing meetings might be as brief as ten minutes, but for big Academic Choice projects, such as those that culminate entire units, the meetings might extend over several sessions (particularly in upper grades) so that everyone has an opportunity to present. Although representing meetings can be the only form of reflection for a given Academic Choice, they often happen in conjunction with individual reflection or with partner sharing.

There are several ways for students to share work during representing meetings:

- Simultaneous display

- Museum walks

- Individual presentations to the whole group

No matter what format you choose, keep in mind that public sharing of work is always a choice. Part of the value of Academic Choice is that students might choose to try out new—and difficult—ideas or skills. If you require students to share the results of experimental work, regardless of the outcome, they will be less likely to take risks and will lose a wonderful opportunity for growth.

Simultaneous display

In a simultaneous display, students sit in a circle. All who wish to share their work hold it up or place it on the floor in front of them. The teacher provides a focus, such as looking for new ideas, to guide the group in purposeful observation. Simultaneous display allows everyone to have their work seen for a moment and to see and gather ideas for future projects. Because no individual is singled out from the others, this strategy provides an emotionally safe way for less confident children to begin to share their work publicly.

Museum walk

In a museum walk, students display their work around the room, then walk around and quietly observe all the work. The teacher can give a focus for children to think about as they look at each other's work, such as "See how many different ways we found to show the number 12." The walk may conclude with a few children offering questions and comments for anyone in the group or with some students sharing their responses to the focus question.

Individual presentations to the whole group

Again, students gather in a circle. The presentation begins when a child moves from his or her place in the circle to the designated presentation spot. I usually use a "presenter's chair." Having a special chair for presenters conveys a message of honor and respect. I often designate my chair as the presenter's chair, then I move to another location in the circle. Other teachers might prefer to set aside another chair.

Typically, three or four students take turns sitting in the presenter's chair. The presenter always starts with a brief, general description of the work she is sharing (e.g., "This is my word-find puzzle with all the spelling words hidden in it"). She then responds to the teacher's focus question, which might be about either the product or the process. As the presenter talks, she holds up her work so that all can see it. When she finishes her brief presentation, she asks the assembled group for a few questions and comments and then responds to them. Over the course of a school year, all students will have many opportunities to present their work in this way.

In order for individual presentations to be successful, students need to know how to present material, look and/or listen with care, and respond thoughtfully. As with all the other aspects of Academic Choice, it's important to start slowly and take time to teach and practice routines.

- Establish and teach routines for presenting to a group. For children to present their work successfully, they need practice in speaking clearly, presenting focused information, looking at the audience members, initiating questions and comments, and responding to audience questions. You can provide this practice in early Academic Choice experiences and during Guided Discoveries. Also, if you do a *Responsive Classroom* style Morning Meeting, the sharing component provides great practice in presenting to an audience. For more information on sharing during Morning Meeting, see *The Morning Meeting Book* by Roxann Kriete. (Kriete 2002)

- Establish and teach routines for asking questions and making comments. When presenters finish their brief presentation, it's time for questions and comments from the audience. Questions and comments are required, not optional, because they provide the social interaction that fosters deeper learning. In addition, a child who receives no response from classmates is likely to feel discouraged, if not embarrassed.

  The audience members should not raise their hands until the question-and-comment time. Their job during the presentation is to listen carefully. If they raise their hands during the presentation, they are possibly thinking more about their question than about what the speaker is saying. Also, raised hands can distract speakers, particularly inexperienced ones.

  The presenter needs to signal that it's time for questions and comments. A good way to do this is with a phrase such as "I'm ready for questions and comments." In addition to marking the end of the presentation period, the words "I'm ready" also say, "I expect there will be questions and comments."

- Teach students to ask respectful questions. Paying careful attention and then generating thoughtful questions and empathic comments takes practice and some structure. One way I've helped students learn and practice good questioning skills is to present something really boring and then challenge them to come up with respectful questions.

"I've been practicing handwriting," I might say. "This is my page of *a*'s." I'm ready for questions and comments."

They come up with ideas such as "Which one is your favorite *a*?" "How long did it take you to do it?" "Did you have to sharpen your pencil a lot?" "Will you practice more letters tomorrow?" "Do you like handwriting?" "Is this your favorite thing you did today?" "When did you first learn how to make an *a*?"

Reflecting
Phase of
Academic
Choice

- Teach students to make comments that show interest. Typically, children will think of questions more readily than comments. To help them think of good comments, I'll return to my "boring presentation" of writing the letter *a*. First, I'll model how to make a comment: "You must really be patient to write a whole page of *a*'s!" or "You must feel proud that you did that."

   Then I'll ask students to think of some other respectful comments, and we'll generate a list together. The list may include comments such as "I notice that your letters are really neat," "You must feel happy to be finished," "Handwriting is hard," "Handwriting is fun," or "You worked really hard."

- Post a list of questions and comments for future reference. It can be helpful to record and post the list of questions and comments generated in response to such challenges. Students can then refer to the list when they need ideas for questions and comments. Other teachers have found it helpful to post the words *who, what, when, where, why* as reminders for different ways to ask questions. Another idea is to post sentence starters such as "You must feel . . ." and "I notice . . ." When students rely on prompts, their questions and comments might seem mechanical rather than spontaneous for a while. But the prompts provide powerful scaffolding that allows the children to participate constructively in the meeting. As they gain experience, their responses will become more original and spontaneous.

   No matter how much you practice generating good questions and comments, children will still fall back on responding with a simple compliment: "I really liked your story." This is a nice comment but not very useful. Comments serve as important feedback, so they need to carry specific information. To make this kind of response more useful, you can teach the presenters to thank the commenter and then say, "What do you like about it?"

Individual reflection and self-evaluation

Students also need time for private reflection without an audience in order to think freely about their experiences and their work. They may write or draw their thoughts in response to open-ended prompts or questions, or they may form judgments of their work in relation to a set of criteria as a form of self-evaluation. Individual forms of reflection may occasionally replace representing, but more often they occur in addition to representing.

Teachers provide a focus for the individual reflection, just as they do for representing, although the focus might consist of a series of open-ended questions or sentence starters, rather than one question. As with focus questions in representing, individual reflection questions should help students think concretely and deeply about their work and the process of the work.

Teachers can write questions or sentence starters on the board (particularly in upper elementary grades), or they can construct a worksheet. If students are making written plans in the planning phase, reflecting questions or sentence starters can go on the back of the planning sheet.

When my students work on choice projects that take more than one session to complete, I often have them spend a few minutes writing their reflections at the end of each session. I can read these reflections later to help me keep track of how the students are doing, and I often write brief notes on each set of reflections as a way of maintaining a personal connection and providing encouragement for each student. The following day, the children read my responses to their reflections along with their original plans as a reminder and motivator for continued work. Reflections written at the completion of an activity also serve as a record of accomplishment and growth that can be collected in portfolios and possibly shared at parent conferences.

Self-evaluation

By evaluation, I mean rating, grading, designating rubric scores, or otherwise attributing a score to the quality of student work according to some external criteria. Self-evaluations can address both academic goals and social skills such as sharing, giving help, or following directions. Teachers select the criteria they want their students to think about and ask them to communicate how well they met the criteria. Although such evaluation is never a part of the more public, social realm of representing, there are times when self-evaluation (as opposed to teacher evaluation) is a useful structure for individual reflection.

The most appropriate time for self-evaluation is when choice activities demonstrate mastery of knowledge or skills. Students evaluate where they stand in regard to externally generated requirements and standards and where they could improve. Self-evaluations may be oral or written. When they are written, teachers may add their evaluations alongside the children's.

Oral self-evaluations

Oral self-evaluations are most useful at the end of simple, brief choice lessons. Teachers gather their class and ask a question such as "How well did you accomplish the goal of learning to spell the words when you did

Reflecting Phase of Academic Choice

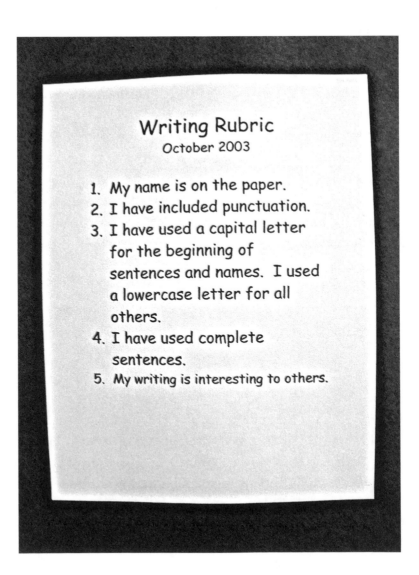

Writing Rubric
October 2003

1. My name is on the paper.
2. I have included punctuation.
3. I have used a capital letter for the beginning of sentences and names. I used a lowercase letter for all others.
4. I have used complete sentences.
5. My writing is interesting to others.

your choice work today? Thumbs up if you think you met the goal; thumbs down if you don't think you did." Students then display the thumbs up sign if they feel they did well and thumbs down if not. A second part to this exercise might include having children turn to a neighbor and explain why they gave thumbs up or thumbs down.

Written self-evaluations

For written self-evaluations, students could use a rubric to guide them as they examine their work and how they went about it, and then they could write where they think they fall on the rubric and why. Teachers might develop the rubrics, or they might take them from a curriculum guide. Teachers and students might also work together to develop rubrics as part of the introduction and planning stage of the choice lesson. Teachers may also create forms for written self-evaluations based on criteria they establish (either by themselves or in discussion with students) or on curriculum frameworks and standards. (For examples of self-evaluation forms, please see Appendix A.)

Focus questions in reflecting

Simply sharing work is usually not enough to promote the kind of thinking that helps children build memory and learn in a meaningful way by making connections to personal experience and to past learning. To think about their work in productive ways, they need a focus for reflection.

Many teachers use open-ended questions to provide a focus for reflection. Good focus questions refer to children's concrete experiences rather than to abstract ideas. They push students to think in depth about their work and then articulate those thoughts. They do not ask students to rate their work or compare it to others' work. The goal is to deepen thinking, and this is much less likely to happen when the focus is on evaluation or competition. On the next page, you'll find sample focus questions.

Reflecting Phase of Academic Choice

Sample questions about work products	Sample questions about work process
■ What is one thing you like about your work? ■ What do you most hope that others will notice about your work? Why? ■ What is one thing you learned from doing this work? ■ What would you do differently if you could do this work again? ■ What would you do next if you had more time to work on this? ■ What is your favorite part? Least favorite part? ■ What is one thing that surprises or interests you about your work?	■ Which of the spelling words (math problems, vocabulary words, characters, etc.) did you find hardest to do using your chosen method? What made it hard? ■ What helped you concentrate/made it hard to concentrate? ■ How did a classmate help you? ■ How did you help a classmate? ■ Did you finish? Why or why not? ■ What was one problem you had? How did you solve it?

You can assess the quality of a focus question by the quality of the responses it generates. Does the question lead to personally meaningful responses that students can back up with specific, concrete examples, or does it lead to rote and obvious answers? Fifth grade teacher Sharon Ralls used Academic Choice when she wanted her students to demonstrate what they had learned during a science unit on energy. Her focus question for their representing meeting was "What do you think you could do to improve your work?" Here are some of their responses:

- Keep projects simple. Don't try to add too many details.

- Give yourself about five minutes to get started. If ideas don't come easily, switch to another activity.

- When you're finished, help someone else.

- Stay on task. Don't fool around.

- Remember what's most important about the project.

- Remember to share and cooperate.

Chapter Five

In general, the more abstract the question, the less thoughtful or engaged the responses will be.

Following are examples of both poor questions and thought-provoking questions.

Reflecting Phase of Academic Choice

Poor questions	Thought-provoking questions
How does your work show you met the lesson goal? *"I met the goal because I spelled the words."*	What is one thing you learned? *". . . that a lot of the words have silent e's."*
What makes your work good? *"I met the criteria for good work."* *"I scored a 4 on the rubric."*	What do you like best about your work? *"I blended the colors/spelled all the words."*
What would improve the Academic Choice lesson? *"Better choices." "Less noise."*	What can you do to make your work better? *"Concentrate." "Get tools ahead of time."*
What do you think about how you behaved today? *"Okay." "Some kids were wild."* *"I don't know."*	What did you do to help classmates? *"Work quietly." "Share ideas." "Clean up."*

In Mr. Kenyon's room—the reflecting phase in action

Beginning with a simultaneous display of work

Mr. Kenyon's fourth graders sit in a circle. Mr. Kenyon raises his hand in a signal for silence and waits. Once all the children are silent and looking at him, he speaks. "Everyone place your work on the floor in front of where you're sitting so that we can all see it. As always, you may choose not to share your choice work." Two hesitant students quietly put their work behind them, while the rest of the class places their work on the floor.

Mr. Kenyon chooses to use a representing meeting format, which he begins with a simultaneous display of work. He reminds his students that public display of work is always a choice, and two choose not to share their work. This may have been because they did not feel good about it, because they were not finished and preferred to wait until they were done for others to see it, or because they were simply not yet comfortable having their work on public display.

Students share reflections with a partner

"Let's just be quiet a minute and look around at all the different ways you found to practice your spelling words using writing, or drawing, or word-find puzzles, or cutting and pasting. See if you can find an idea that you might never have thought of yourself." Mr. Kenyon pauses for a minute as the students look around at each other's work.

"Now turn to your neighbor and take turns telling one thing you like about your work and one thing you like about their work." From silence, the children's voices rise to soft, hesitant whispers. As more and more begin to speak to each other, their voices rise in volume until Mr. Kenyon sits amidst a chattering group. From his seat, he listens to some of their conversations.

"I like that I got a lot of letters cut out," says Jason. "And I like all the letters you put in your word-find puzzle. You made it tricky."

His partner, Ramon, responds, "Yeah, I like how big my word-find puzzle is. I didn't know if I could get it all done, but I did. And I like all your letters too. You have a lot of a's!"

"Well, I have to, because there are a lot of a's in the spelling words."

To respond to Mr. Kenyon's question, the children needed to look at the work carefully, identify specific components and attributes, and then articulate their thoughts. Mr. Kenyon had his class do this partner sharing so that they could practice skills they'd need for the more formal presentations to follow, but he could have chosen to end the meeting at this point.

Mr. Kenyon also wanted his students to develop a basis for judging their own work. Rather than ask them questions like "What makes work good?" or "Is your work good?" he asked, "What do you like about your work?" Students needed to look at the work they had produced with some sense of critical awareness, focus on the details, and name what they valued. As they shared their ideas about their own work and their partner's, the children developed a broader sense of what they value that might help them judge and discuss the quality of their work more readily in the future.

Three students present their work to the group

Reflecting Phase of Academic Choice

After a couple of minutes, Mr. Kenyon raises his hand in a signal for quiet again. "We have time for three people to present their work. Here are two questions for you to answer when you present. The first question is 'Are you finished with your work?' The second question is 'What is one thing you did that helped you finish or that made it hard to finish?' Take a minute to think about what you might say, then raise your hand if you'd like to present your work."

Mr. Kenyon calls on Nicky, then vacates his chair and moves to another place in the circle. Nicky brings her drawings to the presenter's chair vacated by her teacher. She holds up a large piece of drawing paper with the spelling words listed in colorful, patterned letters. She has created a different pattern for each word.

"I did drawing and I used lots of different colors and designs," Nicky tells the group as she displays her work by showing it first to classmates to her right, then slowly around the rest of the circle. "I finished it and one thing that helped was I just used designs, like stripes and polka dots. You can do them pretty fast. I'm ready for questions and comments." She looks around the circle of children as several hands go up. "Charla?"

"I like the one where you did the yellow zigzags. It looks cool."

"Thank you," Nicky says, and then calls on James, her tablemate.

"How did you think of all those different designs?" he asks.

"I don't know, I just did. Ummm, I kind of doodled and got ideas." Nicky calls on Shayna.

"I really like it," Shayna tells her.

"Thank you. What do you like about it?"

"I like that you finished it and you did different designs."

"Thank you, Nicky. Who else is ready to present?" Mr. Kenyon says, as Nicky returns to her seat in the circle. He looks for a volunteer who chose something besides drawing. Seeing Latisha's raised hand, he calls on her.

Latisha settles into the presenter's chair and displays her word-find puzzle slowly around the circle. The square grid she outlined for the puzzle fills most of the sheet of graph paper. Ten spelling words, some of them used twice, are arranged inside the grid. Many empty squares remain.

"I made a word-find puzzle and it was hard because I had a lot of squares to fill in," she says. *"I didn't finish it yet because I have to write all the words twice, then I still have to fill in the other squares with some other words and letters to make it hard. But I'm almost finished writing the spelling words two times each. I'm ready for questions and comments."*

Latisha calls on Janine who asks, "Why did you do all the spelling words twice?"

"Well, I needed to fill up the squares and I want it to be a hard puzzle and Mr. Kenyon helped me think of doing the spelling words twice," she replies, and then calls on Tivon.

"I think it will be a hard puzzle when you're done. Are you going to let someone solve it?"

"Yeah, if they want."

Many hands wave in the air, and Mr. Kenyon reminds Latisha, "You can call on one more person."

Latisha looks around with a grin and calls on Marcus.

"Did you like making it?" he asks.

"Yeah, except it took longer than I thought."

"Thank you Latisha. One last presenter." Mr. Kenyon looks around the circle as Latisha returns to her seat. "What about someone who did cutting and pasting?" He calls on Marcus, who takes the presenter's chair and displays his page of cut-and-paste spelling words.

"I finished it and I spelled all the words and I got it all done because me and Stacy helped each other find the right letters in the magazines. I'm ready for questions and comments." He calls on James.

"I notice that some of the letters are little and some are big."

"Yeah," Marcus chuckles. "We just cut out any letter that we needed to spell the word, so they look funny."

"Was it hard to get all the right letters?" Jason asks next.

"Not too hard because we just looked at a word and found the letters for just that word and when we had that word spelled we looked at the next word, and we shared our letters," Marcus replies, nodding toward Stacy. He calls on Leeanne.

"I like the way you made lines with a ruler so that the words were all straight."

"Thank you." Marcus returns to his seat.

"It's time to get ready for math, now," Mr. Kenyon tells the group. *"First go back to your work areas and put away the materials you were using for spelling practice. If you haven't finished your spelling work, you can do it when you get some time later today or for homework. If you do it for homework, check in with me about taking home any materials you need."*

Mr. Kenyon decided to have his students focus on processes that helped or made it difficult to complete their work. As he observed the students during the working phase, he noticed that some had developed strategies, either purposely or by accident, that allowed them to practice spelling all the words in the designated time, whereas others were using approaches that made it unlikely they would finish during the work time. Some needed to develop more awareness of how their processes affected their ability to meet the goal of the lesson and what they could do to improve.

Fine Tunings

When he first introduced representing meetings to the class, Mr. Kenyon modeled his expectations by presenting a piece of work he had done. He asked the group what they had noticed about his presentation, then he had them brainstorm ideas for how they might present, in a similar manner, another work sample he had prepared. They also brainstormed several possible responses to different focus questions. Students practiced presenting, in pairs, a piece of their own work to each other while Mr. Kenyon circulated and gave them feedback. Finally, he gave all children a turn in the presenter's chair to practice presenting a piece of work they had each done. He gently redirected them if they gave more than a sentence or two as a general description (unless they were reading a written piece) and reminded them when they forgot to respond to the focus question. After a while, this routine was second nature.

Mr. Kenyon often limited each presentation to three questions or comments in the interest of staying on schedule, but not always. Sometimes, especially when students shared larger, more long-term projects, he allowed more than three questions and comments, and sometimes, when time was short, he allowed only one or two.

FINE TUNINGS

Q. *I find that the same few children always volunteer to present or offer questions and comments during representing meetings.*

A. First and foremost, continue to focus on developing a safe and inclusive sense of community in your classroom so that more and more students will be willing to take the risk of speaking at meetings. Other strategies can be helpful from time to time. Sometimes I have children present in alphabetical order. They can pass if they wish, but if this is the routine and they know what to expect, they are often more willing to present. During the working phase, I sometimes invite certain children who don't usually present to do so and help them rehearse what they might say. Children who are hesitant to volunteer are often eager to accept an invitation.

You can also invite certain children to ask questions and make comments in advance and alert the presenter to be sure to call on one of these children along with two others chosen by the presenter. This could become part of the ritual of asking for questions and comments. Another strategy is to have representing meetings in small groups occasionally and either spread the dominators out among the groups or place them together in the same group. Either way, more children will have time to speak.

Q. *Even though I've taught children to ask respectful questions and make positive comments, some children still make sarcastic or hurtful ones from time to time.*

A. Once you have taught students how to ask respectful questions and make positive comments, don't hesitate to use logical consequences if children ask questions or make comments that are intended to hurt or embarrass another child. Children must feel emotionally safe to expose their work and their thoughts to the group.

Q. *Why didn't Mr. Kenyon have the children focus on whether they met the learning goal rather than on what they liked about their work and whether they finished it?*

A. The most accurate assessment of how well the children learned to spell the words will come in the post-test as well as in the children's use of the words in daily writing. Mr. Kenyon is assessing what the children are learning as he interacts with them during the work time. To ask children to reflect on whether they achieved the learning goal of mastering the spelling of the words could be problematic for several reasons:

Fine Tunings

- Such a focus asks children to rate their learning on the key measure set by the teacher. A negative answer implies failure and a positive answer implies success, but neither response promotes deeper thinking or the attachment of personal meaning to the experience. Children may well feel pressure to claim that they did learn the words without actually looking back carefully on what they learned.

- It is a difficult question for the children to answer honestly at that point. They will not know if they have mastered the spelling of the words until they've had a chance to see if they spell the words correctly on post-tests or in the context of daily writing tasks. Rather than grounding the reflection in concrete actions and products, children are being asked to make an abstract generalization that they are not prepared to make honestly.

- Part of the power of Academic Choice is that it supports children to set personally meaningful goals in addition to the curriculum goals set by the teacher. Combining goals that are important to individuals with goals that are important to the curriculum can lead to learning that reaches far beyond curriculum goals. Many of the focus questions that are most effective ask students to think about what *they* value and find challenging about their work.

- The best questions for focusing student reflection ask students to choose, describe, and express opinions about concrete products and behaviors. If teachers decide they want children to focus on how correctly they are spelling, the teachers need to provide a concrete context that truly allows the students to see, measure, and form a personal conviction based on observable evidence. For example, in Mr. Kenyon's lesson, children could certainly report on whether they had opportunities to practice spelling the words correctly and what helped or didn't help them to do so.

Proponents of developmentally appropriate learning assert that how we learn is as important as what we learn. In other words, the process is as important as the product. Mr. Kenyon was honoring this principle when he asked his students to consider the processes they used to complete the activity even if they were unable to finish it in the time allotted. Greater awareness of how they are, or are not, accomplishing goals will eventually lead to a greater rate of meeting the learning goals of the activities.

Works Cited

Johnson, D. B. 2003. *Henry Climbs a Mountain.* Boston: Houghton Mifflin Co.

Kriete, Roxann. 2002. *The Morning Meeting Book.* Greenfield, MA: Northeast Foundation for Children (NEFC).

Rogoff, Barbara. 1990. *Apprenticeship in Thinking: Cognitive Development in Social Context.* New York: Oxford University Press USA.

Vygotsky, L. S. 1978. *Mind in Society: Development of Higher Psychological Processes.* Cambridge, MA: Harvard University Press.

Chapter Five

Letter-Writing Literacy Choices

- Remember to finish unfinished work before making a new choice.

1. Write a new version of The Jolly Postman.
2. Write a new version of Dear Mr. Blueberry and tell a story through letters.
3. Read one of our letter writing books and complete a response form.
4. Write a letter to...
   - George Bush (Dear President Bush,)
   - Phil Bredesen (Dear Governor Bredesen)
   - Bill Purcell (Dear Mayor Purcell)

   Mr. Durnan
   Ms. Touchstone
5. Play Reading Bingo with the letter-writing books.

PART THREE

TEACHER PLANNING FOR ACADEMIC CHOICE LESSONS

In Parts One and Two, I've presented numerous examples of Academic Choice lessons in action. Clearly, these lessons don't just happen magically any more than a non-choice lesson does. To run smoothly, Academic Choice lessons require planning. Teachers need to decide which lessons will work well as Academic Choice lessons and then think about the goals of the lesson, choices to offer, timing and structure of each phase, management considerations, and assessment methods. For teachers new to Academic Choice, this might seem daunting. But it doesn't need to be. In Chapter Six, I'll take you step-by-step through my own planning process as I plan a lesson for fifth graders who are beginning a new novel, *Bud, Not Buddy*. In Appendix A, I offer many specific ideas for lesson plans and activities.

Incorporating Academic Choice into the curriculum

Many teachers worry that they'll have a hard time fitting Academic Choice into an already full schedule. It's important to remember that Academic Choice is not an add-on but rather a strategy that you can use to structure many types of required lessons and activities.

You can incorporate Academic Choice into many portions of the school day. To figure out where you might use Academic Choice, it might be helpful to think about three broad purposes for using Academic Choice:

1. Learning new skills and/or information
2. Practicing new skills
3. Demonstrating mastery of content or skills

Teacher Planning for Academic Choice Lessons

Learning new skills and/or information

When children are learning new skills and/or information, they might choose *how* to learn and/or *what* to learn. If I wanted to plan an Academic Choice lesson with a goal of learning basic information about insects, for example, I could decide to have children choose *how* to get some initial information and then share what they've learned. Possible options might include reading about insects in a book or on a website, listening to a recording or live person tell about insects, conducting an interview with someone who studies insects, observing and recording insects' appearance and behavior, or watching a video. I could also have all the children learn some basic information about insects and attributes they share, and then have each child choose *what* kind of insect to study in more depth.

Practicing new skills

There are many occasions in school when children need to practice in order to gain greater fluency with certain skills or sets of information. For example, students may have recently learned about using dictionaries to find the meanings of words. For an Academic Choice lesson, children could choose to play a word game; look up words in the dictionary and then draw their meaning; or look up words in the dictionary and pantomime their meaning for a partner. These are all choices of *how* to practice.

Choices of *what* to practice may also be effective. Children might choose which vocabulary words to practice based upon interest or on which words are less familiar to them. They can choose what problems to solve, or what reading comprehension strategy to practice among those they have learned.

Demonstrating mastery of skills and/or content

Once students have had opportunities to learn or review information, teachers can use Academic Choice to structure opportunities for synthesizing and expressing that knowledge. Fifth grade teacher Karen Baum had her class choose ways to show what they had learned during a unit on women gaining the right to vote. Some made Venn diagrams showing the rights of men and women during the era just before women's suffrage; some created comic strips that told of the events leading up to suffrage. Others created magazines dedicated to the women's movement of the time or wrote letters that referred to women gaining this right from the point of view of a person living during this era. All of these options allowed children to choose *how* to share their knowledge and understanding. Children might also choose *what* key concepts and facts to demonstrate from among a list of the learning objectives for the unit.

Choosing an appropriate lesson for Academic Choice

As they begin implementing Academic Choice, teachers sometimes ask me if they can structure regular lessons as Academic Choice lessons. The answer is a qualified "yes." You can structure many regular lessons as Academic Choice lessons but not all.

There are two important considerations. First, can students take a variety of paths to meet the learning goals of the lesson? An early step in planning an Academic Choice lesson is to create a list of ways children might meet the lesson's goals. If you can think of three to five choices that will address a range of learning styles and needs, then that might be a lesson that will fit the Academic Choice structure. But it's not a good idea to create a list of options just for the sake of offering choice. A good question to ask is "Will the possible choices offer opportunities for meaningful learning and growth?"

The second consideration is to think about the prior knowledge and skills students will need in order to do the varied activities. Do all students have the necessary experience with techniques and materials? You might have a great idea for an Academic Choice lesson but have the lesson fall flat because students don't know relevant background information or have the skills needed to do focused research or write a persuasive paragraph or use markers to make a poster. Students need a lot of preparation in order to make choices and work independently. (See Part One.)

Keep these considerations in mind as you think about the following two sources for lesson ideas.

Teacher Planning for Academic Choice Lessons

Look at regular lessons and activities that include choices

Many teachers already provide choices for routine activities and lessons. During writing time, students might choose what to write about or a genre in which to write. For reading practice, students choose books they will read for independent reading. Often teachers have children choose a science or social studies topic to research and then demonstrate their knowledge in some way such as a report, poster, or model. Activities such as these provide a great way to begin using Academic Choice. The choices are already in place so teachers need only develop the phases of planning, working, and reflecting.

Consider curriculum guidelines

Taking a look at state curriculum guidelines and learning objectives might point you toward appropriate lessons. For example, Massachusetts mathematics curriculum framework K.N.1 requires kindergarten students to learn to count by 1s to at least 20. (Commonwealth of Massachusetts 2000) As I think about it, this objective immediately suggests a number of activity choices. Children could count each other, snack items, seconds, steps, Unifix cubes, buttons, blocks, pennies, and an infinite number of other things. Academic Choice is a great way to meet this learning goal.

Another Massachusetts curriculum framework for grades 1–2 asks students to "Identify, reproduce, describe, extend, and create simple rhythmic, shape, size, number, color, and letter repeating patterns." (Commonwealth of Massachusetts 2000, Standard 2.P.1) Choices are named as part of the objective itself! After initial instruction in recognizing and extending patterns, children could choose whether to practice recognizing and extending patterns using sound, pattern blocks, or drawings. When they present their work to each other during the reflecting phase, they will learn different ways of showing patterns and in the process, reinforce the basic concepts. Academic Choice promises to be an engaging, efficient, and effective way of addressing this goal.

Here are some other learning objectives that lend themselves to the structure of Academic Choice:

- Build or draw geometric objects. [Choose an object, choose a medium]

- Identify and build a three-dimensional object from a two-dimensional image of that object. [Choose a medium for building, e.g., Legos, modeling clay, paper, blocks]

- Understand how to use metric measurement. [Make a scale drawing where one centimeter = one meter, create a treasure map using metric measurements, create word problems that must be solved by the use of metric measurements]

- Identify common themes among folktales from different heritages. [Choose a folktale to read, choose a theme to seek out]

- Identify the use and meaning of metaphor in literature. [Choose a metaphor or a piece of literature, choose a way to express the meaning of a metaphor]

- Practice reading sight words [Use flash cards, play a matching game, write and say the words, or draw illustrations for each word]

- Learn to construct a paragraph. [Choose a topic]

- Learn the names and locations of the states of the United States. [Create a puzzle, trace a map, fill in names of states on outline map, play Game of the States™ or Name That State™]

In Appendix A, you will find a variety of examples of Academic Choice lesson plans to help you get started.

Work Cited

Commonwealth of Massachusetts. Department of Education. 2000. "Interactive Mathematics Curriculum Framework." Online. http://www.doe.mass.edu/frameworks/math/2000/ Accessed October 2004.

Chapter Six

CREATING A LESSON PLAN FOR ACADEMIC CHOICE

It's a few days before my fifth grade class is scheduled to begin reading a new novel, *Bud, Not Buddy*. (Curtis 1999) I have before me a list of the Massachusetts curriculum frameworks for the study of fiction in grade five (Commonwealth of Massachusetts 2004) and a copy of the novel. Standard 12 states that students need to be able to identify the important elements of a story such as character, setting, and plot. Standard 8 says that students should be able to identify and draw conclusions based on the author's description of setting, character, and event.

With these standards in mind, I reread the first chapter of the book. The author introduces Bud, the main character, indirectly, by describing events, objects, his thoughts and actions, and the actions of the people around him. Although the author tells the reader a lot of information, the reader needs to look for clues in order to form a good picture of Bud. I decide that this poses a perfect opportunity to help my students develop the ability to understand important elements of fiction, character, and setting by making inferences based on specific text. Using clues provided by the author, the children will essentially need to generate a direct description of the character, the setting, or both using their own words and images.

I quickly think of a variety of media that the children could use to do this:

- Writing—The students have recently practiced writing descriptive paragraphs, and this would offer a great opportunity to apply this skill.

- Drawing—Many children in the class like to draw, and drawing a character within a setting could be a wonderful way for them to express the images suggested by the author.

- Cut-and-paste collage—I can also envision how children could cut out illustrations from magazines that would represent various aspects of character or setting and put the illustrations together in a cut-and-paste collage.

- Found poems—We've also done some work this year with "found poems." (Janeczko 2000) I wonder if students could portray elements of character or setting by creating a found poem, using actual phrases from the chapter. It would be fun to try!

As I think of all these ideas, I realize that this will be a great lesson to structure as an Academic Choice lesson. Academic Choice might help the students begin the study of a new book with excitement, creativity, and investment. Perhaps, when the students have choices about how to depict their understanding of character or setting, they will develop a greater curiosity and affinity for the book than they might have otherwise. I'm excited about the possibilities and ready to begin planning.

Creating a Lesson Plan for Academic Choice

Planning a lesson for *Bud, Not Buddy*

In this chapter, I will consider, in detail, the process of planning an Academic Choice lesson. In addition to explanatory text, I will also continue the story of my own planning for the *Bud, Not Buddy* lesson.

Steps in the Planning Process

Step 1: Establish activity objectives based on learning goals and establish preliminary criteria for good work.

Step 2: Decide what choices to offer.

Step 3: Set up and schedule the sequence of the lesson.

Step 4: Proactively consider management issues.

Step 5: Establish evaluation procedures.

Step 6: Determine what materials are needed.

Step 1: Establish activity objectives based on learning goals and establish preliminary criteria for good work

Once I've decided on a lesson to structure as an Academic Choice lesson, I need to establish learning goals and criteria for successfully meeting those goals. Developing more specific, concrete activity objectives helps me identify the aspects of a lesson that are amenable to Academic Choice and those that are not. And establishing the preliminary criteria for good work makes the goal even more specific and concrete. Let's return to my example of planning a lesson on the novel, *Bud, Not Buddy,* to see how this plays out.

Establish activity objectives

In my initial planning, I determined that the students would use textual clues for understanding important elements of character and setting. But what, specifically, will they need to do to meet this goal? First, I realize that the cover illustration offers important information about Bud that is not included in the first chapter (for example, it shows that Bud is an African-American boy, a fact not mentioned either directly or indirectly in the first chapter). So, I make a note to take a look at the cover with the students before they read the chapter.

Next, they will need to read the chapter carefully and identify words, phrases, sentences, and/or passages that offer clues about Bud and about the setting. The students have some experience doing this from past reading lessons, but they have always done it with my direct support. They will probably need a review before I send them off to do it on their own. They will also need to know the meaning of all key vocabulary, so I make a note to skim the chapter and identify words or phrases that some children may not understand. Once they've identified the clues, they'll need to put the clues together and infer a description of Bud and of the setting for the story.

With these specific objectives in mind, I look at the first chapter again. I find at least twelve clues about character but only four subtle clues about the setting. I'm concerned that using clues to infer setting will be too difficult a task for the students to do independently, so I decide to work together with the children to find and use the setting clues. This way they'll learn about the setting and gain further experience with finding and using textual clues.

I now have specific activity objectives for the lesson: Students will examine the cover and read the first chapter of the book with understanding; identify clues the author and the illustrator provide about the main character, Bud; and then communicate their impressions of his character.

Establishing preliminary criteria for good work

Next, I ask myself, "How will I and my students know to what degree they have met the goals and objectives of the lesson?" I decide:

1. Students should locate at least six clues about Bud's character.
2. They should write down the clue and the page number so that they can easily find the clue again.
3. They should construct an image of Bud that reflects all the information given in the clues they recorded.

If these three criteria are met, then I know that students understand the basic process and can document their work.

Step 2: Decide what choices to offer

Creating a Lesson Plan for Academic Choice

The objectives and criteria represent requirements for the children's work. Within these limits there is plenty of room for students to exercise their own initiative and judgment. In the *Bud, Not Buddy* example, the children can choose which six clues to record, and they can choose how many clues above the minimum number of six to find and record. Finally, they can choose how to show their understanding of Bud's character.

I will offer them a range of activities to choose from for describing Bud, so my next task is to plan these activities. When I plan activities, I try to offer some variety so that students with a range of talents and interests and moods are likely to find one activity that appeals to them. On the other hand, because I want children to make purposeful choices, I limit the number of options. Research has confirmed the human tendency to make more random decisions when confronted with a large number of choices than when confronted with a smaller number. (Iyengar and Lepper 2000) I usually try to offer somewhere between three and six options as a general rule.

Teachers sometimes ask children to generate activity ideas. For this to work, it's best to wait until both teacher and students feel comfortable and successful with teacher-generated choices. When I include children in this part of the planning process, I offer two or three options that I've planned, and then during the introduction to the Academic Choice lesson, I open the floor to the children's ideas. I share the goal of the lesson, list the options I've selected, and clarify what materials are available, then ask, "What are some other ways you could meet this goal?" Sometimes children have wonderful ideas that would never occur to me!

Planning activities that support successful completion

When I first conceive of a lesson, I often think of a list of activities that I can offer as choices. Because I want students to complete the activities independently and successfully, I now measure these ideas against two factors—students' prior experience with the activity and their knowledge and skills.

To see this in action, let's go back to my planning session for *Bud, Not Buddy*. I initially thought about offering choices of writing, drawing, creating "found poetry," and making a collage. I'm also considering two more options: making three-dimensional representations and acting out something about Bud's character. The following describes my thinking as I consider each option more carefully and make a final decision about including it (+) or excluding it (-).

+ *Writing a descriptive paragraph*

My first idea is that children can write descriptive paragraphs. They have recent experience with this form of writing and can work independently. In addition, they will have an opportunity to practice this skill in a different context. I decide this is a good option.

+ *Drawing a picture of Bud*

Next I consider the option of drawing. At first, this seems like an obvious choice but as I think about the information available in the first chapter, I realize that students will learn mostly about Bud's history or character traits (for example, he's kind to young children and he treasures his cardboard suitcase). Do the children have the necessary drawing skills to represent these things? I try to imagine final images. They could draw Bud holding the suitcase in his arms and smiling at a smaller child. I imagine how other attributes might be symbolized as well, and soon I am convinced that drawing is a viable option, but I make a mental note to brainstorm ideas for drawings when I introduce this activity.

+ *Creating a "found poem"*

I like the idea of creating a "found poem" using words and phrases from the text. But will some children just string words together without thinking about sound or imagery? I decide to create my own poem about the setting. I list words and phrases that have to do with setting, then try arranging some of them in different sequences. I realize that it's the rearrangement that is the key to creating an effective poem. I could cut strips of paper, and individuals could write one phrase on each strip, then play around with different arrangements before writing down a final poem. This experimentation might increase the likelihood of thoughtful work. I decide that I'll share my poem about the setting and limit the number who can choose this option to five. That way I can observe the poetry writers more closely and be sure to give them extra support if they need it. I am curious how it will work out.

+ Making a cut-and-paste collage

Making cut-and-paste collages is another option. Students have done cut-and-paste collages for other assignments. I imagine what they might do for this option and try out my ideas. Yes, this will work and now I have a model to share when I introduce the cut-and-paste option.

Creating a Lesson Plan for Academic Choice

− Making three-dimensional representations

Next I consider whether there are ways students could use modeling clay to make three-dimensional representations of Bud's character. We've done a Guided Discovery of modeling clay, and they've used it for several other activities. But it's hard for many of the students to show fine detail with modeling clay so I decide this is not a good choice.

− Acting out an aspect of character

I also wonder whether students could act out important aspects of Bud's character. But we haven't done much dramatization yet. Before they can be successful with this as an independent choice, they'll need more structured experience. I make a note in my planning book to incorporate dramatizations into other non-choice assignments further into our study of *Bud, Not Buddy*.

I have a final list of choices to present: writing a descriptive paragraph, drawing, writing a found poem, and making cut-and-paste collages. I also have examples of two of the choices. From past experience, I know that I need to have a very good idea about how my students might actually use the different media I consider. In some cases, I could do this with a little thought; in other cases I need to try the ideas out for myself. By trying the ideas out, I can be sure they will work; I can prepare ideas in case my students need help getting started; I can create models to share with them and stimulate their own ideas; and I can determine what types of guidelines, limitations, and materials might be needed for that option to work to meet my goals.

Step 3: Set up and schedule the sequence of the lesson

With a list of choices in place, the next step is to set up and schedule the sequence of the lesson, beginning with any activities needed to establish the background knowledge, then deciding how the students will plan, work, and reflect on their choices. This is the stage of planning in which I figure out how to put into action all the thinking I've done in previous steps.

For the *Bud, Not Buddy* lesson, I know I want to fit the entire lesson into fifty-five-minute sessions on three consecutive days. On Monday and the first twenty minutes of Tuesday's work session, I'll introduce the book, do any needed background work, and introduce the choices. In the second part of Tuesday's session, students will think about and make their choices. On Wednesday, they will do their work and then reflect on the work. Children who aren't able to complete their work during the time allotted on Wednesday will be able to finish it up as homework and turn it in by Friday.

Setting the stage

Whenever I plan student choice activities, I note the skills and knowledge students will need in order to complete the activities independently. Although I won't offer a choice that requires extensive prior teaching, I sometimes need to review skills or give background information or demonstrate a variation on a previously learned technique. I usually do this in work sessions that occur before the Academic Choice session. In planning the *Bud, Not Buddy* lesson, I decide to take all of Monday's session and part of Tuesday's session to set the stage.

On Monday, I'll introduce the book and essential vocabulary. Then I'll give them time to read the first chapter. On Tuesday, we'll work as a group to identify clues about the setting of the book and infer a description of the setting. I'll lead the whole class in finding clues and list them on the board. Then I'll have the students share their ideas about the setting in pairs before sharing with the whole group.

Introducing the choice activities

As soon as I feel confident that the children have the knowledge they need to complete the choice activities, I move toward introducing the Academic Choice part of the lesson. This often flows smoothly from the setting-the-stage phase. On Tuesday, the second day of the *Bud, Not Buddy* lesson, I plan to go directly from working with the class on describing the setting to introducing the choice activities.

As soon as the children finish sharing their ideas about setting, I'll tell them they will use the same strategies to find clues and make inferences about the character of Bud. Then I'll introduce the choices they have for activities along with the models I created for the found poem and the cut-and-paste options.

Finally, because I have noticed that many of the children seem to choose activities based on what their friends choose, I plan to lead a brief discussion on the pros and cons of making choices this way. I don't want to give children the impression that there is something wrong with making choices based on friends' preferences. Friends can offer inspiration and support that increases learning and satisfaction. But when students only consider their friends' preferences, they might miss out on opportunities to expand horizons, take on challenges, and develop their own set of interests and skills. So, I'll tell them I want them to consider other ways they might make their choices.

Creating a Lesson Plan for Academic Choice

Scheduling and organizing the student planning phase

At this point, I need to figure out how children will make and record their choice activity. I want to encourage thoughtful, independent choices, so knowing the group's tendency to follow their friends, I decide not to go with my usual strategy of having students sign up on a chart. Instead, I plan to hand out scrap paper while the children are still sitting in the circle for the introductory meeting. I'll ask them to think quietly to themselves about which activity they would like to choose and then write it on the paper. When they hand the paper in to me, I will dismiss them to get ready for lunch.

Scheduling and organizing the working phase

When I plan the working phase, I think about how long students will need to complete the tasks, where they will work (at usual seats, at stations, at self-chosen places), and with whom they will work (alone, in assigned pairs or groups, in self-selected pairs or groups). Factors that influence these decisions include the nature of the activities, access to materials, the nature of the group, and whether activities will be messy to do, or require extra setup or cleanup. Over the years, I've found that the more time I spend clarifying goals and thinking through my choices, the easier it is to make decisions about the working phase.

How long will students work?

For the *Bud, Not Buddy* lesson, I plan to spend much of the reading session on Wednesday working on choices. Students will have only forty-five minutes to find at least six clues about Bud in the text and create the images of him. But children need to be able to work at different paces, especially when they're working on creative projects. Some are very efficient and turn out complete, high-quality work in a short time. Others need time to think and move at a slower pace to do their best. I decide that the bulk of the work will be done on Wednesday but that the deadline for complete work will be a couple of days after the working session. I will advise them to complete unfinished work for homework, or during the times between arrival and Morning Meeting.

Will students work alone or with partners?

At first, I'm not sure whether students should work individually or with partners. On the one hand, working individually will help them focus on positive aspects of their choice activity other than collaborations with friends and will give me more information about their individual skills. But since time is also a consideration, I decide to assign students to partners for finding the clues. This will provide support for those who may find this task difficult. After recording clues, they will work on their choice activities as individuals. I take a few minutes to make the partner assignments and add a note reminding myself to talk about this subject when I introduce the choices.

Where will students work?

Since none of the choices requires special materials or workspaces, students can sit in their usual seats, except for the poetry writers. I want them to sit together so that I can keep a closer eye on them and provide more consistent support. Also, if they sit together, they will probably help each other. I decide to designate the reading group table for those who are creating found poems.

When will students clean up?

I also need to think about when children will clean up. Cutting and pasting will require more cleanup than the other options. Rather than have those children stop earlier than the others, though, I think I'll wait until after the representing meeting for cleanup and encourage everyone to help with cut-and-paste cleanup when they've put away their own materials.

Scheduling and organizing the reflecting phase

There are several decisions I need to make as I plan this phase: Do I want to include self-evaluation in the reflection process? Do I want the children to reflect individually? As a group in a representing meeting? Both? If I decide on a representing meeting, how will I structure and focus the process?

Will students engage in self-evaluation?

In planning the *Bud, Not Buddy* lesson, I decide against self-evaluation. I want students to stay excited about the process of learning new skills and am concerned that self-evaluation will slow their momentum and inhibit their excitement. Self-evaluation is most appropriate when the goal of the lesson is demonstration of mastery. At this stage, it's my job to observe and assess progress, not the students' job.

Will I offer representing or individual reflection?

The choice between representing and individual reflecting is less clear. Representing meetings offer a great structure for developing and expanding children's ability to reflect constructively on their work. They learn from each other as they see and think about a range of ways to approach a task. The advantage of individual reflection is that everyone has a chance to reflect actively on their work, not just those who present to the group. Sometimes, after a complex Academic Choice project, I might combine individual reflecting and representing, but for this lesson I opt for just doing a representing meeting. I want them to see and think about a wider variety of clues in the text than they might have found on their own as well as a wider range of ways to demonstrate what they know about Bud.

How much time should I allow for representing?

Next I consider the timing. If I plan on ten minutes for pairs to find six clues about Bud and thirty minutes for individuals to work on their images of Bud, I should have about ten minutes for a representing meeting and five minutes for cleanup.

What is the focus of the representing?

Finally, I construct focus questions for the representing by going back to my goal for the lesson. Possibly the biggest challenge for the students will be finding ways to show some of the more abstract attributes of Bud. I write a pair of focus questions for the meeting: "What clue about Bud's character has been hardest to show in your project? How are you showing it?" Now my plan is set.

Step 4: Proactively consider management issues

No matter how experienced the teacher and how brilliant the lesson, something can and will present problems. Throughout the planning process, I think about potential problems and adjust my plans to address those problems. For example, in the *Bud, Not Buddy* example, I knew that the students relied too much on choices that friends make, so I structured the student planning process to support another way of making choices. I also considered the problem of one group needing more time for cleanup and of children working at different paces.

But even though proactive management is an ongoing consideration as I plan, I find it's helpful to pause at this point and review my goals and my plans. I think about past difficulties or concerns and consider what difficulties might arise in this particular lesson. How have I addressed the potential problems? Are there problems that I haven't thought about?

Looking at my *Bud, Not Buddy* plan, I'm concerned that there may be some students who just don't understand the task and who identify irrelevant passages as ones that give information about Bud. If this happens, of course, it will give me some good information about who needs more work with this skill, but I do want to set them all up for success as much as possible. My plan to work as a group on identifying passages that give information about the setting will help avoid this problem. Maybe I should also make a point of identifying one or two passages that are irrelevant as well and have a discussion about why they are irrelevant. I make a note to add this to my introduction.

Step 5: Establish evaluation procedures

Next, I want to plan how I will evaluate the children's progress. Assessment, as with all aspects of lesson planning, begins with a clear articulation of learning goals. Some of the goals will be specific to the particular lesson, and some will be goals that I might apply to many lessons in many subject areas. For example, the goals of care and punctuality in creating final products apply to much of the work that children do.

Asking questions to guide teacher observation

The primary mode of assessment used for any Academic Choice lesson is embedded assessment in the form of teacher observations and notes that are guided by the goals. In planning assessment for the *Bud, Not Buddy* lesson, I know that academically I want the children to develop their skills in identifying key aspects of text and using them to make inferences about the important element of character. Socially, my most specific goal is that the children practice making choices about the activities they will pursue based on their own interests rather than on what their friends are choosing. I ask myself what other important goals I hold for this lesson and realize that I also hope that students will be engaged in their work and motivated to think hard and do their best. I hope they will interact with each other in friendly and respectful ways as they plan, work, and reflect. These are goals that hold true for any work they do in school.

Creating a Lesson Plan for Academic Choice

What are my specific questions?

My experience tells me that expressing my goals as questions will best guide my observations. Here are questions I list for the *Bud, Not Buddy* lesson:

- Can students identify key words and phrases that provide information about the character of Bud?

- Can they use the textual clues to make accurate inferences about Bud?

- Can they use their selected media to communicate effectively what they have learned about Bud?

- Does it seem that fewer children made choices based on the choices of friends than in the past?

In addition to these lesson specific goals, I'll observe whether students are being friendly with each other, staying on task, persisting in problem solving, working independently, and taking care with their final products.

I copy the questions down so that they will be handy during the lesson to guide my observations of the children as they plan, work, and reflect. I leave space after each question so that I can jot down notes about my observations. I also like to provide extra space to record other observations that are not directly related to the questions. For example, as I observe the children writing their choices down, I might notice that someone seems very indecisive. I might take note of special skills or interests individuals display as they work or reflect, or of unexpected problems that arise.

What do I want to think about later?

After the cycle of student planning, working, and reflecting is complete, I can take my observation notes and use them to reflect on how the lesson went and directions I would like to take in future Academic Choice sessions. These reflections can take many forms, but I find the following questions useful:

- What were the strengths of this lesson?

- What concerns do I have about the implementation of the lesson?

- What concerns do I have about the outcomes of the lesson?

- What might I do differently in a future Academic Choice lesson?

Sharing criteria for good work with the students

Next, I create a final set of criteria for good work to share with the children during their introduction to this Academic Choice lesson. After reviewing my initial criteria, I create the following list:

- I listed at least six clues from Chapter One and included them in my image.

- This work could give someone who didn't read the chapter a good idea of what we know about Bud.

- This work shows my own original ideas.

- I completed this work by the deadline.

- My work is neat.

- Most words are spelled correctly.

I write these criteria on chart paper that I can post when I introduce the choices to the children.

Incorporating student self-evaluations

At times teachers feel a need to record a grade or rating of some sort for students' Academic Choice work. Written student self-evaluations provide this kind of assessment and allow the students to feel a continued sense of ownership and intrinsic motivation. If desired, teachers can add their evaluations to those of students.

Should I include student self-evaluation in this lesson?

In the *Bud, Not Buddy* lesson plan, I do not include self-evaluation because the students are developing new skills. But if I were planning this lesson at the conclusion of their studying the novel, I might ask them to review the entire novel and then name ten to twelve of Bud's most important characteristics. I could have offered them the same choices for showing their understanding of Bud's character but I would expect their work to show mastery of the content rather than progress in developing skills and I would ask them to evaluate what their work shows about their learning.

To structure the self-evaluation process, I ask students to use the criteria for good work as a guide while they rate themselves on a rubric. In addition to the ratings, I ask students to write an explanation of why they rated themselves as they did.

I could use either a general rubric or a rubric designed specifically for the lesson. On the facing page is a rubric specific to a full unit on the *Bud, Not Buddy* novel.

How accurately do students assess their own work?

When students first begin to complete self-evaluations, they often exhibit one of two common tendencies. Either they are too harsh on themselves and rate themselves lower than they actually deserve, or they are too easy on themselves and rate themselves higher than they deserve. Many students have little or no experience with formal evaluation of their own work, and it may take a while to figure out how to do it well and to trust that teachers will not punish them as a result of honest responses. Including the teacher's rating and comments alongside the student's rating brings balance to the evaluation and provides more objective feedback for students. I find that over time, students' self-evaluations more closely reflect my evaluations.

Creating a Lesson Plan for Academic Choice

Self-Evaluation

Topic: _____

Student Name: _____

Date _____

Next to each statement below rate yourself from 1 to 4 with 4 meaning you did an excellent job with the criteria in the statement and 1 meaning you did a very poor job with that criteria. Then write an explanation of why you rated yourself as you did.

Student	Teacher	
		I listed at least 10 different characteristics of Bud that came from different chapters in the book.
		This work could give someone who hadn't read the book a good idea of what Bud is like.
		This work shows original ideas.
		This work was completed on time.
		I concentrated on my work most of the work period.
		I was friendly and respectful of classmates while planning for, creating, and reflecting on this work.
		This work is neat and all the words are spelled correctly.

Overall rating for this work:

Teacher comments:

Chapter Six

There are times when a student's ratings and comments also provide me with important information. A student who seemed to me to have been quite friendly and helpful to classmates may give herself a low rating on this criterion and explain that she made an unkind remark to her tablemate about her work. Another student's self-evaluation might reveal that he put much more effort into his work than I realized when he explains that though he did not concentrate well during the work session at school, he took the assignment home and worked on it for an hour that evening.

Step 6: Determine what materials are needed

To finish my planning, I check that I have all the materials I'll need for the Academic Choice project. With specific options in mind, I consider what materials to gather and what limits to set upon their use. I review notes that I've made during the planning process and make a detailed list of what I'll need to gather and prepare.

Gathering materials for the *Bud, Not Buddy* lesson is fairly straightforward. Writing a descriptive paragraph only requires pencils and paper, but I think I'll also gather some examples of descriptive paragraphs that I used when I first taught this skill. For the found poems, I decide to bring index cards rather than take the time to cut strips of paper. Markers, colored pencils, and crayons along with drawing paper are already out on shelves as is colored construction paper and stacks of old magazines for those who choose to draw or make collages.

The finished plan

As my planning time draws to a close, I finish my planning for the *Bud, Not Buddy* lesson. In all, it has taken me about one hour. The result is a complete and detailed lesson plan that will effectively guide me—and the students—through a successful Academic Choice experience. Here's what the *Bud, Not Buddy* lesson plan will look like. (A blank copy of the lesson plan format is available in Appendix A.)

Academic Choice Lesson Plan

Topic: Reading Chapter One of *Bud, Not Buddy*

Purpose: *(learning new knowledge or skills, practicing new skills, demonstrating mastery)* Practicing the skill of using textual clues to infer information

Learning goal: Develop students' ability to gain understanding of important traits of a character (Bud) by making inferences from clues in the text and illustrations

Activity objectives: Students will understand key vocabulary, read the chapter, identify relevant clues provided in the text, and use the clues to infer a description of Bud.

Criteria for good work:

1. At least six clues listed, with page references
2. A final image created that uses inferences from listed clues and conveys a good idea of Bud to someone who hasn't read the chapter
3. Original ideas
4. Work completed by deadline
5. Neat work; correct spelling

Choices: (what or how)

What (content)	How (process)
Students may choose which clues to include Students may choose how many clues to include above the minimum number	Students may choose a medium to use to create their description from the following options: 1. Write a descriptive paragraph 2. Create a found poem 3. Draw a picture of Bud 4. Make a cut-and-paste collage

Planning: *(oral, sign-up, choice board, written)* At the end of the introduction on Tuesday, I'll hand out slips of paper. Students will write their choices on the slips and return to me.

Working: *(Where will students work? Assigned or student choice? With whom will students work? Individually, partners, groups? Teacher assigned or student choice?)*

During reading period on Wednesday, students will work in regular seats. They will work in assigned partners to find clues (10 minutes) and individually to create the descriptions of Bud (30 minutes).

Reflecting: *(How will students reflect? In a representing meeting, in writing, by self-evaluation? What is a possible focus for reflection?)*

The representing meeting will take place in the last ten minutes of Wednesday's session; three students will present.

Possible focus for reflection—What clue about Bud's character is hardest to represent in your description? How did you solve this problem?

Classroom management considerations: *(What are some potential issues that might come up as students work on this Academic Choice project? How can I address those issues proactively?)*

Potential issues	Ways to address issues
Students make choices based on what friends choose.	Lead a discussion about making choices independently vs. making choices based on friends' choices and encourage students to make choices differently than in the past. Have students make choices in writing rather than publicly on a sign-up chart.
Some students might not finish work during Wednesday's session.	Establish a Friday deadline. Students can complete work as homework or before lessons begin in the morning.
Some students might identify irrelevant passages.	Model how to identify relevant and irrelevant passages. Pair students who are having difficulty with this task with students who are doing it with ease.

Preparation: *(What will I need to prepare to introduce the lesson? What will I need to prepare for each phase? What materials will students need? What is already available? What prior knowledge do students need? How will I introduce the lesson?)*

Materials to prepare—Bring index cards

Prior knowledge required—Review how to write found poems; bring model found poem and collages; discuss strategies for representing abstract character traits with visual images.

Introduction—

Monday:

Introduce book, examine cover, teach key vocabulary, read Chapter One

Tuesday:

1. Lead group in identifying relevant and irrelevant text for getting clues about the setting. Have pairs make inferences, then share ideas about the setting. Generate ideas about how to describe the setting.

2. Introduce goal of finding clues about the character of Bud and creating a description of him based on the clues.

3. Assign students to partners for identifying and listing clues.

4. Introduce activity options for independent work with samples of a found poem and a collage. Lead students in brainstorming ways to represent abstract character traits (such as caring) using visual media.

5. Share and post criteria for good work.

6. Discuss reasons for choosing to do a particular activity other than because a friend is doing it and encourage the group to consider different reasons when making their choices.

Assessment of learning: *(How will I assess learning? How will I know if the specific learning goal has been met? What are other criteria for good work? What is a possible focus for teacher observation?)*

Teacher assessment: Observation.

Focus for assessment: What basis are students using for making choices? What difficulties are they having with the tasks?

In closing

Throughout this book, you've seen many examples of Academic Choice in action, ranging from simple spelling lessons to more complex, multiday projects such as the *Bud, Not Buddy* lesson. You've now got the basic tools you'll need to begin implementing Academic Choice in your own classroom. In the appendices you'll find further resources:

- Appendix A, "Ideas for Academic Choice Activities," offers detailed activity ideas and sample lesson plans for a range of activity objectives.

- Appendix B, "Tools for Guided Discovery" gives you a script for a Guided Discovery and a planning sheet.

- Appendix C, "A Word about Open-Ended Choice Periods," gives a brief look at another way of structuring Academic Choice.

- Appendix D, "Resources for Implementing Academic Choice," offers print and Internet resources for more information about offering choice and for useful classroom tools.

- Appendix E, "Research on Providing Choice in Academic Settings," gives more information about studies that look at the benefits of providing choice.

I encourage you to start slowly and build on success. By bringing Academic Choice into your classroom, you will be providing a context and setting for a range of children to work together with a sense of trust and belonging, fun and satisfaction. This is essential to learning. This is how school should feel.

Creating a Lesson Plan for Academic Choice

Works Cited

Commonwealth of Massachusetts. Department of Education. 2004. "Supplement to the Massachusetts English Language Arts Curriculum Framework." Online. http://www.doe.mass.edu/frameworks/ela/0504sup.pdf. Accessed October 2004.

Curtis, Christopher Paul. 1999. *Bud, Not Buddy*. New York: Dell Yearling.

Iyengar, Sheena S. and Mark R. Lepper. 2000. "When Choice Is Demotivating: Can One Desire Too Much of a Good Thing?" *Journal of Personality and Social Psychology* 79(6), 995–1006.

Janeczko, Paul B. 2000. *Teaching 10 Fabulous Forms of Poetry (Grades 4–8)*. New York: Scholastic Professional Books.

Appendix A

Ideas for Academic Choice Activities

When teachers are venturing into new territory, I know that they appreciate specific suggestions and activity ideas. In this appendix, I offer a wide range of activity ideas as well as examples of Academic Choice lesson plans. I've organized the activities and lesson plans according to the three purposes of Academic Choice (see the introduction to Part Three): learning new skills and/or information, practicing skills, and demonstrating mastery of content and/or skills.

I don't intend the lists of ideas to be either exhaustive or prescriptive. You may find some of the suggested choices more appealing and realistic than others. The examples of the learning goals and activity objectives may or may not fit easily into your ongoing curriculum. As you read through my lists, you will probably think of other options for activities that will work well in your setting and with your resources, curricula, and students. I encourage you to use the ideas listed here as a starting point for your own thinking and planning and to make adjustments in both the goals and the activities according to your own needs and best judgment.

You'll find lots of choices listed here. In the early days of implementing Academic Choice, you might want to include only two options, then slowly build up to offering more choices as the children become accustomed to making and acting on their decisions. Optimally, you'll want to offer between three and six choices of activities. Once children are comfortable with making choices, they'll need at least three options in order to feel that they are making truly meaningful choices. But more than six options might be counterproductive because the decision-making phase may become too time-consuming and complex for deep investment in the work itself. (Iyengar 2000)

Activity ideas

As discussed in Part Three, much of what you are already doing in the classroom can be adapted into activities for Academic Choice lessons. As you think about how you currently teach various subjects, you'll recognize a wide range of ways that students learn new information and skills, practice the skills, and demonstrate mastery of what they've learned. In fact, you've probably got more ideas for activities than you can ever use in a year.

On the following pages, I've summarized general activity ideas that might help you develop more specific plans. Some of these general activities are most appropriate for learning new information or skills, practicing skills, or demonstrating mastery but many of them can be used for several purposes. For example, students could write a letter to ask someone for information, to practice writing skills, or to demonstrate mastery of a topic area. In the rest of this appendix, I provide more specific ideas about how to meet activity objectives in several subject areas.

Ideas for Academic Choice Activities

Reading	**Speaking and listening**
<ul><li>Library book</li><li>Textbook</li><li>Website</li><li>Magazine article or newspaper</li><li>Encyclopedia, dictionary, thesaurus</li><li>Brochure</li><li>Handout</li><li>Graph, chart, diagram, or poster</li><li>Documents</li></ul>	<ul><li>Plan and conduct an interview with a knowledgeable person either in person or on the telephone</li><li>Listen to an audiotape</li><li>Listen to a speech or lecture</li><li>Participate in a discussion</li><li>Listen to and watch a videotape</li><li>Learn a song, rap, chant, or poem</li></ul>
Looking, studying, observing	**Manipulating**
<ul><li>Study a map or globe</li><li>Study a picture (painting, photo, illustration, etc.)</li><li>Observe an object closely and record observations (with naked eyes, microscope, telescope, magnifying lens, etc.)</li><li>Observe the behavior of a living thing or things closely and record observations</li><li>Study a display (such as a museum display)</li></ul>	<ul><li>Experiment with different ways to use materials</li><li>Conduct a formal experiment</li><li>Play a game</li><li>Work a puzzle</li></ul>

Writing	Representing graphically
▪ Stories	▪ Map
▪ Various forms of poetry	▪ Flowchart
▪ Scripts/dialogues	▪ Time line
▪ Instructions	▪ Graph
▪ News article	▪ Venn diagram
▪ Persuasive essay or paragraph	▪ Poster
▪ Descriptive essay or paragraph	▪ Chart or table
▪ Journal or diary entries	▪ Web
▪ Memoir	▪ Power Point presentation
▪ Riddles	**Oral presentations**
▪ Comic strip	▪ Speech
▪ Research report	▪ Monologue
▪ Worksheet	▪ Debate
▪ Quiz	▪ Reader's theater
▪ Letter	▪ Script for radio show
▪ New version of a well-known story or fairy tale	▪ Poem or passage of text
	▪ Story
Drawing/painting	**Drama**
▪ Illustrations (comic strip, picture book, brochure, etc.)	▪ Pantomime
	▪ Play or skit
▪ Mural	▪ Student-made video
▪ Still life	▪ Chant or cheer
▪ Scene	▪ Demonstration of skill or process
▪ Card (thank you, friendship, holiday, etc.)	▪ Movement piece
▪ Decorative borders	▪ Living "freeze frame" or tableau
▪ Calligraphy	

Appendix A

Ideas for Academic Choice Activities

Music	**Constructions**
▪ Write and sing a song or jingle ▪ Create and perform a rhythm to express ideas and information ▪ Create and perform a tune to express ideas and information	▪ Game ▪ Puzzle ▪ Book ▪ Maze ▪ Museum display ▪ Brochure ▪ Newspaper ▪ Magazine ▪ Model ▪ Mobile ▪ Diorama ▪ Puppet ▪ Set of cards ▪ Collage

Using Academic Choice to learn new skills and/or information

When you plan Academic Choice lessons with the general purpose of learning new skills and/or information, you want to set the stage for eventual mastery. You'll determine the general topic and the learning goal; students might choose a specific aspect of what to learn and/or how to learn. For example, if students were studying the geography of the United States, I might first introduce the general topic and then allow each student to choose a region or a state to learn about in more detail. In another geography lesson, I might offer students choices of how to learn about geographical landforms (e.g., by reading a textbook, a nonfiction library book, an encyclopedia, or a website, or by watching a video). At the end of each of these Academic Choice lessons, students will share what they have learned. In the process, they can learn more about geography than if everyone explored the same specific content area or read the same textbook.

On the following pages, you'll find a variety of activity ideas for specific objectives in five curriculum areas: reading, writing, mathematics, social studies, and science. These charts are followed by two Academic Choice lessons, written up in lesson plan form.

Curriculum area: Reading

Objective: Retell the main events of a story in sequence

What—choices about content

- Students choose what events are most important.

- Students choose a certain number of main events to sequence from all those in a teacher generated or a student and teacher generated list.

How—choices about process

- Pantomime the main events in sequence.

- Draw pictures of the main events on large index cards and make a mobile with the cards hanging in sequence.

- Draw a map showing where each main event might have taken place and number them in sequence (e.g., for *The Three Little Pigs*, the map would show each of the houses in order or numbered by story sequence).

- Draw and write a comic strip showing the main events in sequence.

- Re-enact the main events using puppets.

- Make a time line of the story events.

- Retell the main events as a storyteller.

- Draw each main event on an index card. Shuffle the cards and arrange them in sequence. Trade sets of cards with a classmate and arrange each other's cards in sequence.

Appendix A

Ideas for Academic Choice Activities

Curriculum area: Writing

Objective: Write a brief research report with a clear focus and supporting details.

***What*—choices about content:**

- Choose a topic or a subtopic (e.g., for a report on Native Americans, choose among several tribes).

- Choose among categories of information (e.g., for a report on a Native American tribe, choose a number of categories among those of food, tools, homes, family systems, beliefs, customs, clothing, etc., about which to gather information).

***How*—choices about process:**

- Choose to take notes on index cards, a structured worksheet, or on notebook paper set up with columns for different categories of information.

- Choose to organize information using a web, an outline, or another kind of graphic organizer such as the outline of a hand with a place to write the category on the palm and one piece of information about the category on each finger.

- Choose to present the report in handwritten or typed format, illustrated or not illustrated, with a decorative cover or without a cover.

Curriculum area: Mathematics

Objective: Create and explore the properties of symmetric shapes.

How—choices about process:

- Use pattern blocks or some other kind of block such as base 10 blocks, unit blocks, Legos™, etc.

- Use watercolors to paint a design on half of a folded sheet of paper that the student then folds so that the painted shape imprints on the opposite side making a symmetric shape.

- Use computer software that allows students to create and explore symmetric shapes (e.g., *All About Shape and Space* from Tool Factory, Inc., www.toolfactory.com).

- Make symmetric shapes out of clay.

- Cut interesting shapes out of construction paper that is folded in half, then mount the resulting symmetric shapes on paper of a contrasting color.

- Design a symmetric pattern for a quilt or a rug using graph paper and markers, colored pencils, or crayons.

- Make a symmetric collage using natural objects such as seashells, pinecones, leaves, pebbles, and twigs.

Appendix A

**Ideas for
Academic
Choice
Activities**

Curriculum area: Social studies

Objective: Learn about the characteristics of desert regions of the world.

What—choices about content:

- Learn about one or more categories of information about deserts and report back to the class (e.g., plants, climate, animals, people, physical features, locations).

- Learn about one desert of the world and report back to the class.

- Generate a list of questions students have about deserts and have them choose one or more to answer.

How—choices about process:

- Consult a textbook, nonfiction book, magazine such as *National Geographic,* or website.

- Study an atlas or map showing locations of deserts or a wall poster or bulletin board display.

- Conduct an interview with someone who has been to a desert.

- Listen to a book on tape.

- Watch a videotape.

Curriculum area: Science

Objective: Learn about the characteristics and formation of the three different types of rocks.

What—choices about content:

- Choose one to three rocks from a collection to identify as metamorphic, sedimentary, or igneous using classroom resources.

- Choose one of three types of rock to learn more about after a general introduction to the three types.

How—choices about process:

- Observe a set of rocks and categorize them by key attributes based on a text or rock identification book.

- Collect a set of rocks and then organize and label them by type and by name using a text or rock identification book.

- Read a nonfiction book about rocks and how they are formed.

- Research websites that give information about rocks and select a few to read.

- Study a geologic map to see where different types of rocks may be found.

- Study a rock collection shared by a local collector, and discuss the collection with the collector.

- Study a poster that shows the rock cycle.

Appendix A

Academic Choice lesson plan for mathematics, grades 3–6

Topic: Ordering fractions

Learning goal: Students will be able to order sets of fractions.

Activity objective: Students will place sets of eight fractions including halves, thirds, fourths, sixths, and twelfths in order from least to greatest.

Criteria for good work:

1. The eight fractions will be placed in the correct order.

2. Students will be able to explain and/or show how they determined the correct order when asked.

Choices: *(what* and/or *how)*

What—choices about content:

Students may choose from one of three sets of eight fractions:

1. 1/12; 1/2; 1/6; 2/3; 5/6; 11/12; 1/4

2. 4/6; 3/12; 1/3; 5/12; 3/6; 3/4; 2/12; 3/3

3. 4/6; 3/12; 8/6; 11/12; 11/4; 2/3; 1/2; 2/6

How—choices about process:

Students may choose among three ways to order the fractions and show their results:

a.   fraction bars
b.   pattern blocks
c.   drawing

Planning: *(oral, sign-up, choice board, written, other format)*

Students place name tags in a labeled basket—First ask students to notice the three sets of fractions and think about which set will be most interesting to work with. When I call on individual students, they will come up to me and point to their chosen set of fractions on a slip of paper I'll hold in my lap. They then put their name tags in a labeled basket placed next to the material they have chosen.

Working: *(Where will students work? Assigned or student choice? With whom will students work? Individually, partners, groups? Teacher assigned or student choice?)*

Students will work in assigned seats. They will work individually.

Reflecting: *(How will students reflect? In a representing meeting, written, self-evaluation? What is a possible focus for reflection?)*

Written reflection

Possible focus for reflection—What was one thing you learned about how to order fractions today that you didn't know before?

Classroom management considerations: *(What are some potential issues that might come up as students work on this Academic Choice project? How can I address those issues proactively?)*

Potential issues	Ways to address issues
Students learn new math skills at different rates. Some will do this task easily; others will struggle.	Offer three sets of fractions, each at a different level of difficulty. Students choose which set to tackle. Encourage students to seek help from classmates.
Students might feel peer pressure to choose either the most difficult or the easiest set of fractions.	Have students report privately which set of fractions they choose. Observe students as they work and adjust the sets of fractions as needed to increase or decrease challenge.

Preparation: *(What will I need to prepare to introduce the lesson? What will I need to prepare for each phase? What materials will students need? What is already available? What prior knowledge do students need? How will I introduce the lesson?)*

Materials to prepare—All materials are in the classroom and available for students' independent use.

Prior knowledge required—How to represent fractions using each of the three materials; how to use the materials to order fractions from least to greatest

Introduction—Before beginning this lesson, students need to know how to use drawing, fraction bars, and pattern blocks to represent written fractions.

1. Post a set of three fractions with mixed denominators. Have students make drawings to represent each fraction and then discuss how they can tell which fraction represents the biggest number and the smallest number. Have them number the drawings from least to greatest.

2. Post a new set of fractions and repeat the procedure above, this time using pattern blocks.

3. Post a third set of fractions and repeat the procedure, using fraction bars.

4. State the goal of the lesson and post the three sets of fractions from which students may choose.

5. Review criteria for good work.

Assessment of learning: *(How will I assess learning? How will I know if the specific learning goal has been met? What are other criteria for good work? What is a possible focus for teacher observation?)*

Teacher will observe during the working and reflecting phases.

Possible focus for teacher observation: What strategies are children using to represent and order the fractions? What aspects of this lesson are most engaging for children? What aspects are most difficult?

Academic Choice lesson plan for reading, grades K–3

Topic: Reading literature

Learning goal: Relate themes of fiction to personal experience

Activity objective: Students will relate a theme of *Henry Climbs a Mountain* (Johnson 2003) to their personal experience. The theme they will relate to their experience is that we can be free through our imaginations. Students will show a way they "escaped" the place where their bodies were by imagining that they were doing something different.

Criteria for good work:

 The goal will be met if students:

1. Show something they created in their own imaginations.

2. Show something they imagined that took their minds to a place that was different from the place where their bodies were at the time they imagined it.

3. Show some details about the imaginary event.

4. Include details that are different from those of other students.

Choices: *(what* and/or *how)*

 ***What*—choices about content:**

No choices

 ***How*—choices about process:**

Students have a choice of how to show what they imagined.

1. Make a picture book about what you imagined.

2. Paint or draw a scene of what you imagined.

3. Make a cut-and-paste collage or picture to show what you imagined.

4. Write a story about what you imagined.

5. Using blocks or modeling clay, make a model of the place you imagined yourself to be.

Appendix A

Planning: *(oral, sign-up, choice board, written)*
Oral

Working: *(Where will students work? Assigned or student choice? With whom will students work? Individually, partners, groups? Teacher assigned or student choice?)*
Students will work individually at assigned seats.

Reflecting: *(How will students reflect? In a representing meeting, written, self-evaluation? What is a possible focus for reflection?)*

Representing meeting. Two or three students present work. All discuss focus question with a partner.

Possible focus for reflection: My favorite part about my work

Classroom management considerations: *(What are some potential issues that might come up as students work on this Academic Choice project? How can I address those issues proactively?)*

Potential issues	Ways to address issues
Some children may have difficulty recalling or creating an imaginary experience and/or some imaginary experiences that children choose to recall may not be appropriate to share at school.	Prepare a guided visualization to use with the children or "pretend" together to be in a different place having an adventure for a few minutes before introducing the choice activities. Have them use the experiences generated in this way for their choice activities.

Preparation: *(What will I need to prepare to introduce the lesson? What will I need to prepare for each phase? What materials will students need? What is already available? What prior knowledge do students need? How will I introduce the lesson?)*

Materials to prepare:

- Prepare a set of blank "picture books" by stapling together pages that each have a space for drawing and lines for writing.

- Blocks, clay, cut-and-paste supplies, drawing and painting supplies, and writing supplies are all readily available for children's independent use in the classroom.

Prior knowledge required:

- Familiarity with the story of *Henry Climbs a Mountain* through student reading or teacher read-aloud.

- Guided Discoveries of the open-ended use of blocks, modeling clay, drawing, and painting materials. Prior experience writing short stories. A model of a completed page or two for the picture book option.

Introduction:

1. Share lesson goals.

2. Discuss times when they might want to free their minds from a situation (e.g., bored, unpleasant work such as clean-up, etc.).

3. Have children tell a partner about a time when their minds "escaped" a situation by pretending they were doing something else and what they pretended. (Circulate and listen to determine the nature and appropriateness of the imaginary events shared.)

4. If necessary, lead the children through a guided visualization to generate a brief imaginary adventure for each one.

5. Present options for sharing imaginary adventures. Share a model of the picture book option and post criteria for good work.

Assessment of learning: *(How will I assess learning? How will I know if the specific learning goal has been met? What are other criteria for good work? What is a possible focus for teacher observation?)*

Teacher will observe.

Possible focus for teacher observation: Are children meeting the criteria for good work?

Using Academic Choice to practice skills

There are many occasions when children need opportunities to practice newly learned skills or to apply new knowledge to various situations. Common instances of topics that require regular practice include spelling, computation facts, vocabulary words and their meanings, or parts of a larger group (e.g., animals, geographic features or places, maps, machines, etc.). Examples of how to practice applying knowledge include organizing things by alphabetical order, using dictionaries, decoding words using short *a* or long *a,* or creating and identifying patterns. Providing choices can make many routine tasks more interesting and meaningful.

Ideas for Academic Choice Activities

Teachers will determine the goals of the lesson; students might choose specific content or a way to practice. For example, given a list of twenty spelling words, students may decide which ten or fifteen of the words they most need to practice. They may also choose how to practice the words from among several choices offered by the teacher. Though they will study fewer words than they would if they were required to learn the entire list, they will most likely be more invested in practicing the words they have chosen and therefore more likely to master their spelling.

Activities for practicing new skills can easily be adapted across a variety of subject areas. For instance, activities for practicing how to find and name the fifty states may easily be adapted and applied to practicing the names of insect body parts. Activities used to practice addition or multiplication facts may also be used to practice recitation of other kinds of facts. Choices about how to practice vocabulary words apply to any subject area that requires learning new terms or words.

On the following pages, I give activity ideas for specific lessons in four curriculum areas: spelling, reading, mathematics, and social studies. I then give two Academic Choice lessons written in the lesson plan format.

Curriculum area: Spelling

Objective: Students will practice categorizing words in a list according to common spelling patterns.

***What*—choices about content:**

Choose what lists of words to categorize.

***How*—choices about process:**

- Write each word on an index card and arrange the cards by categories of words. Have a classmate guess how categories were established. Rearrange the cards into new categories and repeat the guessing activity.

- Make a web or a chart showing all the words arranged by categories.

- Color or decorate words according to shared patterns. For example, all words formed by dropping a silent *e* and adding *ing* are shaded red with yellow highlights.

- Determine two or three patterns shared by several words on a word-hunt list, then look through books and list as many words that share those patterns as you can find.

- Make up a gesture to represent each of the shared patterns, then recite each word while making the gesture for that word's pattern.

- Write each word on an index card, then cut cards into parts with the pattern on one part and the rest of the word on another part (or parts if the pattern occurs in the middle of the word). Mix up the cards and try to reassemble the words.

- Choose a shape to represent each spelling pattern, then draw the appropriate shapes around the words that demonstrate the patterns the shapes represent.

- Make up a rhythmic jingle or chant for the words in each spelling pattern category:

  Shipping, stopping, running, cutting,
  Can't you see
  Bragging, jogging, swimming, hopping,
  Listen to me!

- Use index cards with words on them to play Memory. A matched pair is any two words sharing the same spelling pattern.

Appendix A

Ideas for Academic Choice Activities

Curriculum area: Reading

Objective: Students will gain confidence and fluency in reading text aloud.

What—choices about content:

Choose what to read from among several texts.

How—choices about process:

- Read aloud as part of a "reader's theater." (Each student in a small group reads the part of one character or of the narrator.)

- Make an audiotape of yourself reading a passage from a book, then listen to it.

- Make a "book on tape" of a short story or picture book.

- Practice reading a poem with different tones of voice and expression.

- Read a set of directions aloud so someone else can follow them, or read sets of simple directions and follow them by yourself.

- Choose a passage from a speech or document you like and practice reciting it so that you can read it before an audience.

- Read aloud to a younger child or a classmate.

- Read a list of words or a rhyme while clapping syllables or a rhythm.

Curriculum area: Mathematics

Activity objective: Practice reading and writing two-digit numbers.

How—choices about process:

- Make a set of flash cards by writing a two-digit number on each card, then practice reading the numbers.
- Make a set of index cards with each two-digit number represented twice and play Memory or Go Fish with the cards.
- Arrange magnetic digits, cut-out cardboard or paper digits, or digits written on index cards to make two-digit numbers as a partner calls them out, then switch places with your partner.
- Make up a short story that includes a list of two-digit numbers. Draw a picture about the story with the numbers in it written below, then tell the story to a classmate or teacher.
- Count sets of small objects in containers (e.g., marbles, pebbles, beads, buttons, etc.) and record the number counted.
- Play Number Detectives by finding two-digit numbers around the classroom (e.g., on thermometers, signs, calendars, charts, in books, on maps or globes, on measuring tools, on labels of classroom supplies, etc.). Read and keep a list of them.

Appendix A

Ideas for Academic Choice Activities

Curriculum area: Social studies

Objective: Practice naming and locating the fifty states of the United States (or of a region, the countries of Asia, cities of South America, important rivers and mountain ranges of the world, etc.).

***What*—choices about content:**

Choose what region to study (or what landforms, cities, countries, etc.).

***How*—choices about process:**

- Fill in names on an outline map.
- Copy a labeled outline map using markers, crayons, or colored pencils.
- Put together a puzzle of the topic under study (U.S. map, world map, etc.).
- Color and mount an outline map on cardboard, then cut it into puzzle pieces to reassemble.
- Play a game such as Name That State©, Great States Board Game©, or Game of the States©.
- Create flash cards by drawing the outline of each state on one side of an index card and writing the name of the state on the other side, then use the cards to practice naming the states.
- Use an outline map as a base, and over it build a map out of clay, etching in the outlines of each state (country, city, river, etc.) with a toothpick. Or delineate borders with different colors of clay.
- Use a projector to project the image of a map onto a large sheet of paper, then draw the map on the paper. Post it on a bulletin board without labels and use it to practice naming the states. Refer to a small, labeled map to check for accuracy.
- Trace around puzzle pieces of individual states on construction paper. Cut out the shapes and paste them in place to make a complete map. Add labels that name each state.

Academic Choice lesson plan for mathematics, grades 1–5

(from the faculty of the Lower School of University School of Nashville)

Topic: Computation

Learning goal: Students will communicate their thinking about how they estimate the sums of double-digit addition problems.

Activity objective: Given the problem 54 + 79 = _____, students will estimate the answer and then show how they did so.

Criteria for good work:

The goal will be met if students can:

1. Identify and follow an effective procedure for estimating the sum.
2. Stick with their plan or provide a reasonable explanation for changing it.
3. Create a representation that shows how they went about making their estimate.
4. Explain their representation.

Choices: *(what* and/or *how)*

What—choices about content:

No choices

How—choices about process:

Students have a choice of how to estimate and how to show thinking.

1. How to estimate—Front-end estimation; rounding; breaking apart by number benchmarks 50 + 75, 4 + 4)
2. How to show process—Writing a description; making a flow chart; using base 10 blocks

Planning: *(oral, sign-up, choice board, written)*

Sign-up on board. Teacher pulls names out of hat to establish the order of student sign-up.

Working: *(Where will students work? Assigned or student choice? With whom will students work? Individually, partners, groups? Teacher assigned or student choice?)*

Students will work in regular seats. They will work individually.

Reflecting: *(How will students reflect? In a representing meeting, written, self-evaluation? What is a possible focus for reflection?)*

Representing meeting will take place in the last ten minutes of the session; all students will display their representation; four students will present their representation to the class and take questions and comments.

Possible focus for reflection—What was the hardest thing about doing this work? How did you deal with it?

Classroom management considerations: *(What are some potential issues that might come up as students work on this Academic Choice project? How can I address those issues proactively?)*

Potential issues	Ways to address issues
There is a limited set of base 10 blocks—only enough for six students.	Limit choice of working with base 10 blocks to no more than six students.
None of the three options may appeal to some students.	Ask students to generate one or two other ideas for ways to represent how they went about computing.

Preparation: *(What will I need to prepare to introduce the lesson? What will I need to prepare for each phase? What materials will students need? What is already available? What prior knowledge do students need? How will I introduce the lesson?)*

Materials to prepare—Base 10 blocks, flowchart

Prior knowledge required—The three ways to estimate, use of base 10 blocks, how to make a flowchart, how to write a description of a procedure

Introduction—

1. State goal and present problem.

2. Briefly review the three ways to estimate.

3. Introduce the three choices. Have sample flowchart for estimating a subtraction problem.

4. Ask students for one or two other ideas for ways to represent their thinking process.

5. Share criteria for good work and limits to choices (only six for base 10 blocks).

Assessment of learning: *(How will I assess learning? How will I know if the specific learning goal has been met? What are other criteria for good work? What is a possible focus for teacher observation?)*

Teacher will observe during the working and reflecting phases.

Appendix A

A physical education teacher uses
Academic Choice to structure her class.

Academic Choice lesson plan for mathematics, grades 1–3

(Inspired by a lesson developed by South Brunswick, NJ, first grade teacher Leah Carson.)

Topic: Practice with subtraction

Learning goal: Students will develop fluency with basic number combinations for subtraction.

Activity objective: Students will practice subtracting from numbers up to 10.

Criteria for good work:

The goal will be met if students can:

1. Complete at least eight computations.
2. Use strategies for computing answers to the problems.
3. Explain how the difference was calculated.
4. Give correct answers to most of the subtraction problems.

Choices: *(what* and/or *how)*

What—choices about content:

No choices

How—choices about process:

Students can choose how to practice from a list of five activities that all students have experienced in past lessons.

1. Under the Cup—List of subtraction problems with plastic bears to use as counters. Students count out bears to represent the total number for the problem and then cover the amount to be subtracted with a cup and count the remainder to find the difference.
2. Spinners—Students spin a dial twice and then subtract the smaller number spun from the larger number spun. Counters are available to help with computation.
3. Number Maze—Students practice subtraction with this computer game.
4. Stickers—Given a set of subtraction problems, students use stickers to illustrate the problem and the answer.
5. Bead bars—Students use the bead bars to calculate differences.

Planning: *(oral, sign-up, choice board, written)*

Oral planning. Children announce their choice when called upon.

Working: *(Where will students work? Assigned or student choice? With whom will students work? Individually, partners, groups? Teacher assigned or student choice?)*

Students will work at the tables where the supplies for their chosen activity are located. Students will work individually.

Reflecting: *(How will students reflect? In a representing meeting, written, self-evaluation? What is a possible focus for reflection?)*

Students will share their results in a ten-minute representing meeting at end of session.

Possible focus for reflection—Choose a problem that you found challenging and explain how you got the answer to it.

OR

Was the activity you chose too hard, too easy, or just right? What made it that way?

Classroom management considerations: *(What are some potential issues that might come up as students work on this Academic Choice project? How can I address those issues proactively?)*

Potential issues	Ways to address issues
Popularity of the computer option could lead to disappointment and frustration if all who want to choose it can't.	Offer the computer option only to those who have not yet had a turn on the computer this week. Remind students of other times they can play Number Maze during the day/week.
Students might make choices based on friendships rather than interest in the activity itself, leading them to choose activities that will not best engage them in thinking about subtraction.	During introduction, lead a discussion of what makes an activity "too hard," "too easy," or "just right." Encourage children to choose activities they think they will find "just right."

Appendix A

Preparation: *(What will I need to prepare to introduce the lesson? What will I need to prepare for each phase? What materials will students need? What is already available? What prior knowledge do students need? How will I introduce the lesson?)*

Materials to prepare—Set out materials for each option at different tables.

Prior knowledge required—Experience with each of the choice activities in past lesson.

Introduction—

1. State lesson goal.

2. Announce the possible activities and show a sample of the materials for each activity. Point out the tables where students will go for each activity.

3. Ask for volunteers to briefly describe how to do each activity.

4. Announce who may choose to use the computer for this session and when others will have an opportunity.

5. Share criteria for good work.

6. Lead discussion of what makes an activity hard, easy, or just right and encourage children to consider this when planning.

Assessment of learning: *(How will I assess learning? How will I know if the specific learning goal has been met? What are other criteria for good work? What is a possible focus for teacher observation?)*

Teacher will observe students during the working and reflecting phases.

Using Academic Choice to demonstrate mastery of knowledge and/or skills

Academic Choice can offer students a variety of ways to demonstrate mastery of knowledge and/or skills. Teachers might offer students a choice of what content to focus on. For example, when students complete a unit on the literary genre of tall tales, they might choose three categories of information out of five to include in a final presentation. The categories might include comparisons of characters, settings, use of hyperbole and exaggeration, types of problems and their resolution, and information about the regions where the tall tales originated. When they are able to choose what categories of information they will provide, children are more likely to discover aspects of the content that hold their interest and to develop a more personal connection to that content, which deepens and reinforces learning.

Whether or not children have a choice of what information and concepts to demonstrate, they will benefit greatly if they can choose how they will demonstrate learning. I try to offer options that address as many of the different learning styles and levels of intelligence as possible as long as the choices also suit my learning goals for the project. Not only do such choices reinforce previously learned skills, they also allow children to express their knowledge in ways that work best for them. As a result, their engagement and quality of thinking increase.

Appendix A

For example, after learning how to write haiku, or to make a time line or a web, children might choose to use one of those strategies to show what they know about a historic figure. When students have had plenty of experience with different media and ways of using them through Guided Discoveries and direct instruction, I might simply offer choices of different media and allow the children to decide how they will use the media to meet the activity objectives. For example, if I want children to share information about a geographic region, I might offer the options of drawing, cutting and pasting, blocks, clay, writing, or drama. Those who choose drawing might draw a comic strip, a scene, a picture book, a brochure, a map, or a poster. Other students might use blocks to construct an outline of geographic shapes, construct significant landmarks, or show the sizes of various landmasses to scale.

Before presenting the choices to students, it is important to make sure that they are aware of the criteria you will be using to evaluate their work. You may present criteria for good work that you have developed as part of your lesson planning process, or you may generate the list together with the students as part of your introduction to the Academic Choice lesson. Clarity about expectations will help students make purposeful choices.

Ideas for Academic Choice Activities

Curriculum area: Science

Objective: Show ten important facts that you have learned about electricity.

What—choices about content:

Choice of which ten facts to show

How—choices about process:

- Make a Power Point presentation.
- Make a poster.
- Write a poem or song.
- Make a Jeopardy-type game.
- Make a board game.
- Write a report.
- Make a comic strip in which an expert on electricity demonstrates and explains important facts about electricity.

Curriculum area: Reading

Activity objective: Show ability to create mental images when reading.

What—choices about content:

- Choose what text to read when creating visual images.
- Choose the part of the text for which to show a mental image.

How—choices about process:

- Use watercolors to paint a mental image or scene.
- Use crayons or Craypas to draw a mental image or scene.
- Make a diorama of a visualized scene.
- Write a detailed description of a visualized scene or image.
- Write a descriptive poem.
- Create a tableau that represents the visualized image or scene.

Curriculum area: Mathematics

Activity objective: Show your understanding of what division is and how it works (or of addition, subtraction, or multiplication).

What—choices about content:

Choose among two or more division equations of varying difficulty.

How—choices about process:

- Write a story problem to illustrate the equation.
- Cut and paste shapes to illustrate the equation.
- Use pattern blocks or base 10 blocks to illustrate the equation.
- Use play money to demonstrate how to solve the equation.
- Draw a picture to illustrate the equation.
- Make up a skit that illustrates the equation.

Appendix A

Curriculum area: Spanish

Activity objective: Demonstrate knowledge of key vocabulary and use of conversational Spanish.

What—choices about content:

- Choose among several settings for which to develop a conversation in Spanish.
- Choose what key vocabulary words to include.

How—choices about process:

- Write a story incorporating vocabulary and conversation.
- Make a comic strip that shows a conversation in Spanish.
- Make a picture book.
- Create a diorama of a scene and two characters, then write a dialogue for the characters.
- Create a skit.

Ideas for Academic Choice Activities

Curriculum area: Social studies

Activity objective: Show knowledge about rain forests.

***What*—choices about content:**

- Choose which five rain forest animals, plants, landforms, etc., to show.
- Choose which rain forest to show (e.g., South American, Pacific Island, African, etc.).
- Choose which important concepts about rain forests to show.

***How*—choices about process:**

- Paint a mural.
- Write a travel guide.
- Make a Trivial Pursuit type game.
- Write imaginary journal entries as though traveling through a rain forest.
- Rewrite a well-known folktale (such as *The Three Little Pigs*) and set it in a rain forest with animal characters and types of homes likely to be found there.
- Make a mobile.
- Make a maze that winds through a rain forest setting.
- Construct a model of a rain forest scene.

Curriculum area: Music

Activity objective: Show ability to feel rhythms through music.

***What*—choices about content:**

Choose among pieces of music.

***How*—choices about process:**

- March in time to the music.
- Use rhythm sticks.
- Clap.
- Make marks on paper showing the rhythm.
- Do a dance.
- Use your voice to show the rhythm.

Appendix A

Academic Choice lesson plan for geometry, grades 1–6

Learning goal: Students will build or draw and identify geometric shapes.

Activity objective: Students will demonstrate knowledge of two-dimensional geometric shapes and the names for the various shapes.

Criteria for good work:

1. The final project displays examples of each type of shape studied. (These shapes will vary by grade level.)
2. Student labeled each shape with its correct name.
3. Student stayed on task most of the time.
4. Student completed work by final due date.
5. Work shows thoughtfulness and creativity.
6. Work is neat and easy to read.

Choices: *(what and/or how)*

What—choices about content:

No choices

How—choices about process:

Students will choose how to provide examples and labels for each shape. The choices will be open-ended. Students may choose among the activities listed below or from another idea provided in a student brainstorming session during the introduction.

- Make a picture book that shows and labels the shapes as part of a story or an *I Spy* book.
- Make and label pattern block designs that represent each shape.
- Cut and paste with drawing paper and construction paper to make a chart, scene, or collage with shapes.
- Make a mobile of labeled shapes using chenille sticks and a coat hanger.

Possible student ideas:

- Write "shape poems." (See Janeczko 2000 for a description of this form of poetry.)

- Make a comic strip with shapes as characters.
- Make a game in which shapes must be identified.
- Create a map of an imaginary "shape world."

Planning: *(oral, sign-up, choice board, written)*
   Written plans

Working: *(Where will students work? Assigned or student choice? With whom will students work? Individually, partners, groups? Teacher assigned or student choice?)*
Students may choose where to work. Students will work individually.

Reflecting: *(How will students reflect? In a representing meeting, written, self-evaluation? What is a possible focus for reflection?)*
   A thirty-minute representing meeting will take place on the last day of the project to share and reflect on work; written self-evaluations.

   Possible focus for reflection—How does my work show mastery of the types and names of shapes?

Classroom management considerations: *(What are some potential issues that might come up as students work on this Academic Choice project? How can I address those issues proactively?)*
   A chart on the following page illustrates potential issues and ways to address them.

Preparation: *(What will I need to prepare to introduce the lesson? What will I need to prepare for each phase? What materials will students need? What is already available? What prior knowledge do students need? How will I introduce the lesson?)*
   Materials to prepare—Coat hangers, chenille sticks, copies of *Where's Waldo?* and picture books of shapes as examples for the picture book option

   Prior knowledge required—Guided Discoveries of drawing materials, cut-and-paste materials, chenille sticks, pattern blocks

   Introduction—

   Note: Students have already experienced the Guided Discoveries listed under prior knowledge.

   1. State the goal of the lesson.

   2. Share and post the criteria for good work.

3. Announce the options and provide examples.

4. Ask students for ideas about other ways they could meet the goal for the lesson and add their ideas to the list of options.

5. State limits (e.g., due date, when they can work on the projects, individual work).

Assessment of learning: *(How will I assess learning? How will I know if the specific learning goal has been met? What are other criteria for good work? What is a possible focus for teacher observation?)*
Teacher observation and written student self-evaluation.

> **Possible focus for teacher observation:** What are students showing about their knowledge of geometric shapes? What gaps are there in their knowledge?

Potential issues	Ways to address issues
The students love to work on projects with partners, but group work will make it hard to know if individuals have mastered the material.	Students must plan and complete projects individually.
With open-ended projects, some students may have difficulty planning something they can complete in a timely manner.	Students will complete written plans that I can check. I will make sure they've planned a reasonable amount of work for the allotted time. I can provide two sessions for working on the projects during school and allow students to continue work as homework, if necessary, with a final due date of Friday.
Some students may not have mastered this information yet and will create incorrect products.	Post a chart of the shapes to which students may refer if they need reminders.

Sample student planning sheet
for Academic Choice lesson in geometry,
grades 1–6

Name _____   Date _____

Topic _____

I will _____

Materials I'll need _____

Where I'll work _____

(Draw or write some of your ideas for this project below.)

Appendix A

Sample student self-evaluation form
for Academic Choice lesson in geometry,
grades 1–6

Name_____   Date_____

Rate your work by giving yourself a ✓, ✓+, or ✓– next to each
of the criteria for good work listed below.

_____   I displayed examples of each type of shape we studied.

_____   I labeled each shape with its correct name.

_____   I stayed on task most of the time.

_____   I completed work by the final due date.

_____   My work shows thoughtfulness and creativity.

_____   My work is neat and easy to read.

_____   My overall rating for this work

I gave myself this overall rating because _____

_____

I am proudest of _____

_____

One thing I could improve is _____

_____

Academic Choice lesson plan for reading and writing, grades 3-5

Lesson goal: Students will write a new version of a simple, predictable book, following the format of the initial book, but including their own original ideas.

Activity objective: Students will compose and present an adventure story with a hero or heroine as the main character using the format of *My Father's Dragon.* (Gannett 1987)

Criteria for good work:

1. The story has a hero/heroine as the main character.

2. The hero/heroine has a difficult problem to solve.

3. The hero/heroine solves the problem after undergoing a series of at least three ordeals.

4. Students complete a plan for the story using one of the activities listed below.

5. The story includes some details about:

   - The hero/heroine
   - The setting
   - The problem
   - The ordeals

6. Students present the story in a neat, attractive way.

Choices: *(what* and/or *how)*

What—choices about content:

Within the format of a heroic adventure, students have an open-ended choice of characters, events, and resolutions. *(Beginning*—Introduction of character and setting, introduction of a problem; *Middle*—A series of attempts to solve the problem; *End*—Resolution of the problem)

How—choices about process:

Students choose how to present the adventure story from the activities listed below:

Appendix A

1. Write the story.

2. Make a comic strip of the story.

3. Make a skit with simple puppets.

4. Tell the story on tape.

5. Make a map that shows where the major events of the story take place, similar to the map at the beginning of *My Father's Dragon*.

Planning: *(oral, sign-up, choice board, written)*

Written planning sheets

Working: *(Where will students work? Assigned or student choice? With whom will students work? Individually, partners, groups? Teacher assigned or student choice?)*

Students will work individually at regular seats.

Reflecting: *(How will students reflect? In a representing meeting, written, self-evaluation? What is a possible focus for reflection?)*

Student will have opportunities to present their stories to the class through a series of "Author's Circles" if they choose.

Students will complete written self-evaluations using the attached form.

Possible focus for reflection—See self-evaluation form.

Classroom management considerations: *(What are some potential issues that might come up as students work on this Academic Choice project? How can I address those issues proactively?)*

Potential issues	Ways to address issues
Some children might become so involved in their stories that they go on and on without resolution.	Have the children prepare a plan for the complete story before choosing a way to represent it.

Preparation: *(What will I need to prepare to introduce the lesson? What will I need to prepare for each phase? What materials will students need? What is already available? What prior knowledge do students need? How will I introduce the lesson?)*

Materials to prepare—Be sure there are enough tape recorders and tapes. Gather materials such as craft sticks for making simple puppets. Create and copy blank comic strips for students to fill in. Provide directions for completing each of the activities, either in poster format or as a handout.

Prior knowledge required—Need examples of completed activities for which students might not have models (a page of dialogue for a skit; examples of comic strips).

Children should have prior experience with creating and acting out a short story with simple puppets.

Children should have a basic understanding of what heroes and heroines are and the format of heroic adventures.

Introduction—

1. Describe the goal of the lesson.
2. Review the elements of a heroic adventure using *My Father's Dragon* as an example.
3. Go over the planning sheet with the class.
4. Describe the choices available for presenting their stories.
5. Present the time frame for completing the stories.

Assessment of learning: *(How will I assess learning? How will I know if the specific learning goal has been met? What are other criteria for good work? What is a possible focus for teacher observation?)*

Teacher and student assessment based on the criteria for good work and student's written self-evaluations

Teacher observation of students as they plan and work on their stories

Possible focus for teacher observation: Are students able to complete plans independently? Do they understand the elements of a heroic adventure? Are they engaged in the creation of their stories? Are students discussing their stories with each other? How are students helping each other do their work?

Sample student planning sheet
for Academic Choice lesson in reading/writing,
grades 3–5

Name _____

My hero/heroine's name is _____

Two details about my hero/heroine:

1. _____

2. _____

The setting will be_____

Two details about the setting:

1. _____

2. _____

The problem will be _____

Two details about the problem:

1. _____

2. _____

Two ordeals the hero/heroine will face:

1. _____

2. _____

The hero/heroine finally solves the problem by _____

_____

I will (circle one):

a. Write my story.   d. Tell my story on tape.

b. Make a comic strip of my story.   e. Make a map of my story.

c. Make a skit of my story.

**Sample student self-evaluation sheet
for Academic Choice lesson in reading/writing,
grades 3–5**

Directions: Review the criteria for good work for this assignment. Look at the story you created and think about whether you met the criteria. Then complete this sheet.

My character was a hero/heroine because _____

_____

_____

The best things about my work on this story are _____

_____

_____

_____

One thing that would make my work on this story even better is ____

_____

_____

_____

Appendix A

Additional sample student self-evaluations and a teacher observation format for general use

Sample student self-evaluation #1

Name _____ Topic _____

Date _____

Rate yourself on a scale of 1 to 5 with 5 representing an excellent score and 1 representing a poor score. Use the space below each item to explain why you gave yourself that score.

Ratings   **Criteria**

Student   Teacher

_____   This work is neat and I have spelled words correctly.

_____   I met the criteria for good work for this lesson.

_____   I completed this work on time.

_____   I concentrated on my work and did my best.

_____   Overall score for this work

Teacher comments:

Sample student self-evaluation #2

Name _____ Date _____

(means good work,   means okay work, means poor work)

_____   _____   _____   I concentrated on my work.

_____   _____   _____   I made my work beautiful.

_____   _____   _____   I shared materials when others
                                 wanted me to.

_____   _____   _____   I made thoughtful questions
                                 and comments about other
                                 children's work.

_____   _____   _____   I finished my work on time.

_____   _____   _____   My work shows that I have
                                 learned a lot about this topic.

The best thing about my work is _____

_____

_____

_____

Teacher comments:

Ideas for Academic Choice Activities

Sample teacher observation

1. How are students meeting the academic criteria for good work that I shared with them?

2. How are students interacting in friendly, constructive ways?

3. What do I see that tells whether students are generally on task and taking pride in their work?

4. Other observations:

Sample teacher planning sheet
for Academic Choice lessons

Topic:

Purpose: *(learn new content and/or skills, practice, demonstrate mastery)*

Learning goal:

Activity objective:

Criteria for good work:

Choices: *(List activities available as choices for* what *and/or* how*)*

What (content)	How (process)

Appendix A

Planning: *(oral, sign-up, choice board, written)*

Working: *(Where will students work? Assigned or student choice? With whom will students work? Individually, partners, groups? Teacher assigned or student choice?)*

Reflecting: *(How will students reflect? In a representing meeting, written, self-evaluation? What is a possible focus for reflection?)*

Ideas for Academic Choice Activities

Possible focus for reflection—

Classroom management considerations: *(What are some potential issues that might come up as students work on this Academic Choice project? How can I address those issues proactively?)*

Potential issues	Ways to address issues proactively

Preparation: *(What will I need to prepare to introduce the lesson? What will I need to prepare for each phase? What materials will students need? What is already available? What prior knowledge do students need? How will I introduce the lesson?)*

    Materials to prepare—

    Prior knowledge required—

    Introduction—

Appendix A

Assessment of learning: *(How will I assess learning? How will I know if the specific learning goal has been met? What are other criteria for good work? What is a possible focus for teacher observation?)*

    Possible focus for assessment—

Works Cited

Gannett, Ruth Stiles. 1987. *My Father's Dragon.* Illus. by Ruth Chrisman Gannett. New York: Random House.

Iyengar, Sheena S. and Mark R. Lepper. 2000. "When Choice Is Demotivating: Can One Desire Too Much of a Good Thing?" *Journal of Personality and Social Psychology* 79(6), 995–1006.

Janeczko, Paul B. 2000. *Teaching 10 Fabulous Forms of Poetry (Grades 4–8).* New York: Scholastic Professional Books.

Johnson, D. B. 2003. *Henry Climbs a Mountain.* Boston: Houghton Mifflin Co.

Tool Factory, Inc. 2004. "All About Shape and Space." Software. Available from www.toolfactory.com.

Ideas for
Academic
Choice
Activities

Appendix B

Tools for Guided Discovery

I. Script for a Guided Discovery

This script takes you through each of the steps in a Guided Discovery. Teachers who are new to Guided Discovery often find it helpful to follow the sequence of steps and use the scripted language. To begin the Guided Discovery, gather students in a circle. Small groups might sit around a table.

1. Introduction and naming of materials

> *A. Ask open-ended questions to find out what students already know about the material:*
>
> *What do you know about _____?*
> > and/or
>
> *How have you used _____ in the past?*
>
> Take a few ideas. As students share ideas, introduce or reinforce important vocabulary.

> *B. Ask open-ended questions that help students notice details:*
>
> *What do you notice about the _____?*
> > and/or
>
> *How many different details can you notice?*

> *C. If students need more help with focused observation, ask:*
>
> *What is _____ made of?*
> > and/or
>
> *What shapes/colors/textures, etc., do you see?*

> *D. You might want to walk around with the materials so students can look at them more closely or you might put the materials in the center of the circle so all students can have a good view. Do not hand materials to students at this point.*

2. Generation and modeling of students' ideas

For use and potential

A. Begin with an open-ended question to generate ideas:

How might we use _____ in our classroom?

> or

How might we use _____ to help us with our learning?

B. If student response is slow or if ideas are unimaginative, you could ask:

What new and different ideas can you think of for using _____ to help us practice new learning?

> or

What new and different ideas can you think of for using _____ to help us share something we learned?

Keep asking until you have several student-generated ideas.

**Tools for
Guided
Discovery**

C. Ask a few students to model their ideas using a small set of the materials (write the rest of the ideas on a board or chart).

Ask the first student:

Will you show us how you might do that?

Before s/he begins the modeling, say:

Everyone watch carefully and see what you notice about what s/he does.

The class observes while the student briefly models an idea. During the modeling, ask the class:

What do you notice that s/he is doing?

Write down ideas.

For care during exploration and experimentation

A. Generate ideas about how to care for the material by asking:

What can we do to take care of the _____ when we use them?

B. Gather student ideas then ask one student to model his/her idea:

Will you show us a safe and careful way to take a _____ out and use it?
Before the student begins modeling, remind the class to watch carefully:
Everyone watch carefully and see what you notice about what s/he does.
During the modeling, ask the class:
What do you notice that s/he is doing to care for the _____?

3. Exploration and experimentation

A. Children will work in the circle or at their desks, depending on the age and experience of the children and the nature of the materials being explored. Say:

Now we will all practice using the _____. Begin with this idea. (Or, for a more open-ended exploration: "Try out one of our ideas.")

B. Pass out a limited number of materials to each student. Observe students as they work. Use reinforcing, reminding, and redirecting language as needed to facilitate a positive, successful exploration.

4. Sharing exploratory work

A. If work resulted in a product, say:

If you'd like to share your work, hold it up so all in the circle can see it.
Allow a minute or two for students to view each other's work.

B. If you want to keep the focus on the process of the work, ask:

Who would like to tell one thing you liked about your work?
Call on two or three volunteers. For each sharer, ask for one comment from the group.

5. Cleanup and care of materials

A. Begin by asking a volunteer to model careful cleanup:

Who will show a safe and careful way to put away the _____?
Remind the class to watch carefully:
Everyone watch carefully and see how much you can notice about how _____ cares for the _____.
During the modeling, ask the class:
What do you notice?

B. As the whole class begins to clean up the material, say:

I will watch and notice as you all put away the _____ safely and carefully.

C. Observe students as they clean up. Use reinforcing, reminding, and redirecting language as needed.

II. Guided Discovery planning sheet

Preparation of materials: Write down what you will need to do to prepare the material for Guided Discovery. How will you ensure that children can quickly and smoothly get access to the material? Where will you have them work?

Introduction and naming: Write down what you will say to introduce the material in a way that stimulates interest. What open-ended questions can you ask to invite children to share what they know about the material? How will you get them to look at the material in a new way, noticing new things? What vocabulary do you want to emphasize or introduce?

Tools for Guided Discovery

Generating and modeling of students' ideas: Write down what you will say and do to facilitate children's generating ideas and modeling for use and care of the material:

Exploration and experimentation: Write down what you will do and say to facilitate children's exploration of the material. Where will the exploration happen? What behaviors do you want to reinforce?

Sharing exploratory work: Write down how you will facilitate children's sharing of their work and ideas. How will you focus the sharing?

Cleanup and care of materials: Write down how you will help children think through and practice cleanup and care of materials. What do children need to know? What behaviors will you want to model? Think of the "what-ifs" you might need to address so children can use the materials and solve problems on their own.

Appendix C

A Word about Open-Ended Choice Periods

In addition to the types of Academic Choice described in this book, many K–6 teachers provide students with open-ended choice periods as part of the ongoing curriculum. Teachers use the sequence of planning, working, and reflecting to structure these periods but leave the choices about what students will do during these periods far more open-ended than what is described in this book.

While it's beyond the scope of this book to address how to implement open-ended choice periods successfully, we want to acknowledge the value of this approach and offer resources for those who want to learn more. Open-ended choice periods can be used at any grade level, but it is an especially appropriate structure for the K–1 classroom for three reasons:

- Developing a sense of initiative is important in these two early grades. Open-ended choice periods help young children develop a sense of initiative by providing them with opportunities to exercise their independence and follow their interests within safe boundaries.

- Young children learn best through active exploration of their environment. While older students also benefit from active exploration, most K–1 students still learn primarily through their senses—through what they can directly see and explore for themselves—and open-ended choice periods provide a good structure for this kind of exploration.

- The classroom schedule often can accommodate this structure. Many K–1 schedules already allow for an activity or center time that can be shaped into an open-ended choice period by applying the structure of planning, working, and representing.

In an open-ended choice period, each child can choose a learning area or content area in which to work. While the children work, the teacher observes, facilitates, and supports students' learning.

In a primary grade classroom, children might choose to go to a learning area such as the blocks corner, the drama area, the classroom library, the puzzle corner, the computers, the science area, or the art area. Within each learning area, the teacher arranges materials that have open-ended uses, encourage exploration, support children's interests, and meet curriculum goals. For example, in the science area, the teacher might put out a variety of magnets and materials that might or might not be attracted to magnets. Children who choose to go to this area can explore magnets and make discoveries on their own. Or the teacher might set up the drama area as a post office where children can play out the jobs and roles they have been studying.

Primary grade teachers might also provide specific activities in each learning area, still using open-ended materials. For example, after a field trip to the post office, children who choose to go to the blocks area might have the task of creating the different rooms they visited in the post office. In the science area, after initial exploration with the magnets, children might choose a specific question or problem they want to answer through their exploration and choose a way to show what they discovered.

In upper grades, the children might choose a content area in which to work. Within each content area, the teacher provides a choice of materials to explore or projects to plan and complete. For example, children who choose math might then choose to explore the use of measuring tools, play math games, or practice computation skills.

A Word about Open-Ended Choice Periods

An open-ended choice period has value for many of the same reasons cited throughout this book:

1. It allows children to learn through active exploration of their environment.

2. It supports children's cognitive growth through its structure of planning, working, and reflecting.

3. It helps children exercise independence and initiative within safe boundaries.

4. It allows children to learn at their own level and to learn from their mistakes.

To learn more about open-ended choice periods, please see the following resources:

Bredekamp, Sue and Teresa Rosegrant, eds. 1992. *Reaching Potentials: Appropriate Curriculum and Assessment for Young Children.* Washington, DC: National Association for the Education of Young Children.

Diller, Debbie. 2003. *Literacy Workstations: Making Centers Work.* Portland, ME: Stenhouse Publishers.

Doan, Jane and Penelle Chase. 1996. *Choosing to Learn: Ownership and Responsibility in a Primary Multi-Age Classroom.* Portsmouth, NH: Heinemann.

Dodge, Diane Trister and Laura Colker. 1992. *The Creative Curriculum for Early Childhood*. 3rd ed. Washington, DC: Teaching Strategies.

Dodge, Diane Trister, Judy Jablon, and Toni Bickart. 1994. *Constructing Curriculum for the Primary Grades*. Washington, DC: Teaching Strategies.

High/Scope® Educational Research Foundation, 600 North River Street, Ypsilanti, MI 48198-2898, www.highscope.org. (Offers many resources on providing choice for children, particularly primary grade children.)

Hohmann, Mary and David Weikart. 2002. *Educating Young Children: Active Learning Practices for Preschool and Child Care Programs*. 2nd ed. Ypsilanti, MI: High/Scope Press.

Marriott, Donna, Joel Kupperstein, Gwen Connelly, and Carolea Williams, eds. 1997. *What Are the Other Kids Doing While You Teach Small Groups?* Cypress, CA: Creative Teaching Press.

Mitchell, Anne and Judy David, eds. 1992. *Explorations with Young Children: A Curriculum Guide from the Bank Street College of Education*. Beltsville, MD: Gryphon House, Inc.

Northeast Foundation for Children. 1993. *A Notebook for Teachers: Making Changes in the Elementary Curriculum*. Rev. ed. Greenfield, MA: Northeast Foundation for Children.

Wolk, Steven. 1998. *A Democratic Classroom*. Portsmouth, NH: Heinemann.

Appendix D

Resources for Implementing Academic Choice

Articles

Barclay, K. H. and C. Breheny. 1994. "Letting the Children Take Over More of Their Own Learning: Collaborative Research in the Kindergarten Classroom." *Young Children* 49(6): 33–36.

Cone, J. K. 1993. "The Urgency of Choice in the Untracked Classroom." *Teaching Tolerance* Fall: 57–63. (For middle and high school classrooms)

Howard, R. K. and M. R. Howard. 1997. "What a Difference a Choice Makes!" *Strategies* 10: 16–20. (Choices in physical education)

Jervis, K. 1986. "A Teacher's Quest for a Child's Questions." *Harvard Educational Review* 56(2): 132–150.

Kamii, C. 1991. "Toward Autonomy: The Importance of Critical Thinking and Choice-Making." *School Psychology Review* 20: 382–388. (Theoretical basis for providing choices)

Kohn, A. 1993. "Choices for Children: Why and How to Let Children Decide." *Phi Delta Kappan* September: 8–20.

Turner, J. C. 1995. "The Influence of Classroom Contexts on Young Children's Motivation for Literacy." *Reading Research Quarterly* 30: 410–441.

Books

Allen, I. & Peery, S. 2000. *Literacy Centers: What Your Other Kids Do During Guided-Reading Groups.* Huntington Beach, CA: Creative Teaching Press.

Armstrong, T. 2003. *The Multiple Intelligences of Reading and Writing: Making the Words Come Alive.* Alexandria, VA: Association for Supervision and Curriculum Development (ASCD).

Chase, P. and J. Doan. 1996. *Choosing to Learn: Ownership and Responsibility in a Primary Multi-Age Classroom.* Portsmouth, NH: Heinemann.

Deci, E. L. and R. Flaste. 1995. *Why We Do What We Do: Understanding Self-Motivation.* New York: Penguin Books. (Theoretical basis for providing choices)

Heacox, D. 2002. *Differentiating Instruction in the Regular Classroom: How to Reach and Teach All Learners, Grades 3–12.* Minneapolis, MN: Free Spirit Publishing, Inc.

Janeczko, P. 2000. *Teaching 10 Fabulous Forms of Poetry.* New York: Scholastic Professional Books.

Mantione, R. and Smead, S. 2003. *Weaving through Words: Using the Arts to Teach Reading Comprehension Strategies.* Newark, DE: International Reading Association, Inc.

Vogel, N. 2001. *Making the Most of Plan-Do-Review.* Ypsilanti, MI: High/Scope Press. (For preschool and kindergarten teachers)

Wolk, S. 1998. *A Democratic Classroom.* Portsmouth, NH: Heinemann.

Resources for Implementing Academic Choice

Games and activities

Game of the States. Danvers, MA: Winning Moves. http://www.winning-moves.com/.

Great States Board Game. Parsippany, NJ: International Playthings. http://www.toydirectory.com.

Math War: Multiplication Game Cards. Grand Haven, MI: School Zone Publishing Co. www.schoolzone.com.

Multiplication Rap: CD, Cassette, and Book. Conroe, TX: Rock 'n Learn, Inc. www.rocknlearn.com. (Also resources for practicing telling time, phonics, addition, and subtraction)

Name That State. Rancho Dominguez, CA: Educational Insights. www.edin.com.

Snap It Up. Vernon Hills, IL: Learning Resources. www.learningresources.com. (Multiplication card game)

Websites

Brain Download, LLC. 2004. *Toon University.* www.toonuniversity.com. (Resource for online books and games, teacher resources, and supplies)

Col, Jeananda. 1998. *Enchanted Learning.* www.EnchantedLearning.com. (Offers activities on a wide range of topics, printable books for early readers, and educational software)

The Education Alliance at Brown University. *The Knowledge Loom: Educators Sharing and Learning Together.* http://knowledgeloom.org. (Resource library site where educators can review research and find information on educational practices K–12)

Next Generation Training, Inc. 2003. *EducationalLearningGames.com.* www.educationallearninggames.com. (A resource for buying educational board games from all over the world, grades pre-K–9)

Schools of California Online Resources for Educators (SCORE). 2001–2002. http://www.score.k12.ca.us/. (In addition to a listing of California's educational standards and frameworks, the site offers resources and lesson plan ideas.)

Time Timer, LLC. *Time Timer.* www.timetimer.com. (Time-keeping device to help children self-regulate)

Tool Factory. *Tool Factory, Inc.* www.toolfactory.com (A range of educational software from around the world, K–12.)

Appendix D

Appendix E

Research on Providing Choice in Academic Settings

The following summarizes the findings of thirty-two studies that examined the outcomes of providing choices to students in grades K–12.

I. When students make choices about what and/or how they learn they become more motivated to learn.

- Students are more likely to be on task. They become more engaged in their work, enjoy it more, and feel a greater sense of pride, ownership, and satisfaction. (Rainey 1965; Linn, Chen et al. 1977; Rice and Linn 1978; Jervis 1986; Edwards and Juliebo 1989; Garland 1995; Stanne 1999; McPhail, Pierson et al. 2000)

- They are more likely to incorporate the use of positive learning behaviors and skills at their own initiative than they are when they don't have choices. (Blackwell 1974; Rice and Linn 1978; Amabile and Gitomer 1984; Eriksson 1990; Turner 1995)

- Students who gain more experiences with academically relevant choices tend to prefer more challenging tasks and complete more of those tasks than students who have little prior experience with such choices. (Cosden, Gannon et al. 1995; Glessner 1997; Moes 1998; Jolivette, Wehby et al. 2001; Whalen and Csikszentmihalyi 1991; Umbreit and Kwang-Sun 1996) In one study, students who came from classrooms where they had regular opportunities to make choices were significantly more likely to freely select mathematics problems that provided an optimal level of challenge than were children from classrooms where they did not have regular opportunities for choices. Those children tended to select problems that were either too hard or too easy when given a choice. (Blackwell 1974)

- Choice provision appears to support intrinsic motivation to learn. Students who made choices about some aspects of academic activities were more likely to continue to engage with them during free time than those who were not given choices. Children allowed to select books to read, for example, were more likely to choose to read at other times. Students who chose activities for physical education classes reported more interest in engaging in those activities after school. Researchers also found that students felt a greater sense of competence and self-esteem when they had choices. (Fisher, Blackwell et al. 1975; Eriksson 1990; Cordova and Lepper 1996; Howard and Howard 1997; Condon and Collier 2002)

II. When students make choices about what and/or how to learn, they think harder and use more academic skills.

Research on
Providing
Choice in
Academic
Settings

- In a cross-cultural study, providing choices seemed to enhance problem-solving and critical-thinking skills. Both Anglo- and Asian-Americans who were given a choice of anagrams to solve scored higher on a post-test for solving anagrams than those who were assigned anagrams to practice. (Iyengar and Lepper 1999)

- Another researcher found that when students had choices about what they would read, what information they would use, or how they would complete tasks or solve problems they were significantly more likely to practice reading strategies for decoding and comprehending new texts. These students also showed greater persistence in staying with difficult tasks, and they tended to set intrinsically motivated learning goals (for self-improvement or learning specific content, for example) rather than performance goals (to complete a worksheet or to finish quickly, for example). (Turner 1995)

- Choices also appear to enhance creativity. Young children who were given a choice of materials constructed significantly more creative collages for their art class than those given no choices. (Amabile and Gitomer 1984) In a thinking skills program that provided regular student input into which activities the students would pursue and how they would pursue them, students achieved higher scores of creativity on a post-test than did students in a more traditional, highly directive program. (Eriksson 1990)

- Other researchers have found that choices lead to more self-initiated editing and revision of work; more personal application of learning to students' lives (Glessner 1997); and better organization, understanding, and ability to isolate variables in science experiments. (George 1977; Linn, Chen et al. 1977; Rice and Linn 1978)

III. When students make choices about what and/or how to learn, they are more likely to behave in constructive ways and develop more friendships with a wider range of their classmates.

- In one study of the effects of choices in physical education activities, students reported that they made new friends more often when they chose activities than when they participated in assigned activities. Their teachers reported fewer discipline problems when activities were student selected. (Condon and Collier 2002)

- In an in-depth study of a boy with significant learning and behavior problems, researchers found that his teacher's use of choice was associated with increased friendships and academic performance and decreased problem behaviors over a period of two years. (Jervis 1986)

- Two studies examined the nature of social interactions in classrooms that provided regular opportunities for student input. One found that the students with regular experiences in taking initiative and making decisions about their learning were also more likely to try to solve interpersonal problems through independent discussion and reasoning rather than more authoritarian methods such as tattling or fighting. (Allman-Snyder, May et al. 1975) Another researcher found that first graders who had regular opportunities to make academic choices were also more likely to accept a wider range of classmates as friends than were students who did not have regular opportunities to make academic choices. (Donohue 2000)

- Some of the research on academic choice has focused on students with special needs such as ADHD, emotional disturbances, and other difficulties that are often associated with problem behaviors in school. These studies found that when these students had choices, even limited choices such as which read-aloud story to listen to or which worksheet to complete, the rate of problem behaviors decreased. (Dyer, Dunlap et al. 1990; Dunlap, Kern-Dunlap et al. 1991; Dunlap, DePerczel et al. 1994; Umbreit and Kwang-Sun 1996; Powell and Nelson 1997; Vaughn and Horner 1997; Moes 1998; Peterson, Caniglia et al. 2001) In some cases, the differences were especially dramatic with students' rate of disruptive behavior reduced almost to zero during choice conditions. (Dyer, Dunlap et al. 1990; Dunlap, Kern-Dunlap et al. 1991)

Appendix E

Works Cited

Allman-Snyder, A., M. J. May et al. 1975. "Classroom Structure and Children's Perceptions of Authority." *Urban Education* 10: 131–149.

Amabile, T. M. and J. Gitomer. 1984. "Children's Artistic Creativity: Effects of Choice in Task Materials." *Personality and Social Psychology Bulletin* 10: 209–215.

Blackwell, L. R. 1974. "Student Choice in Curriculum, Feelings of Control and Causality, and Academic Motivation and Performance." School of Education. Palo Alto, CA: Stanford University.

Condon, R. and C. S. Collier. 2002. "Student Choice in Physical Education Makes a Difference." *Journal of Physical Education Research and Development* 73(2): 26–30.

Cordova, D. I. and M. R. Lepper. 1996. "Intrinsic Motivation and the Process of Learning: Beneficial Effects of Contextualization, Personalization, and Choice." *Journal of Educational Psychology* 88: 715–730.

Cosden, M., C. Gannon et al. 1995. "Teacher-Control versus Student-Control Over Choice of Task and Reinforcement for Students with Severe Behavior Problems." *Journal of Behavioral Education* 5: 11–27.

Donohue, K. M. 2000. "Classroom Instructional Practices and Children's Rejection by Their Peers." *Dissertation Abstracts International,* 61 (UMI No. 9979604).

Dunlap, G., M. DePerczel et al. 1994. "Choice Making to Promote Adaptive Behavior for Students with Emotional and Behavioral Challenges." *Journal of Applied Behavior Analysi*s 27: 505–518.

Dunlap, G., L. Kern-Dunlap et al. 1991. "Functional Assessment, Curricular Revision, and Severe Behavior Problems." *Journal of Applied Behavior Analysis* 24: 387–397.

Dyer, K., G. Dunlap et al. 1990. "Effects of Choice Making on the Serious Problem Behaviors of Students with Severe Handicaps." *Journal of Applied Behavior Analysis* 23: 515–524.

Edwards, J. M. and M. R. Juliebo. 1989. "The Effect of Topic Choice on Narrative Writing: Grades 1–3." *English Quarterly* 21: 247–257.

Research on Providing Choice in Academic Settings

Eriksson, G. I. 1990. "Choice and Perception of Control: The Effect of a Thinking Skills Program on the Locus of Control, Self-Concept and Creativity of Gifted Students." *Gifted Education International* 3: 135–142.

Fisher, M. D., L. R. Blackwell et al. 1975. "Effects of Student Control and Choice on Engagement in a CAI Arithmetic Task in a Low-Income School." *Journal of Educational Psychology* 67: 776–783.

Garland, K. 1995. "The Information Search Process: A Study of Elements Associated with Meaningful Research Tasks." *School Library Media Annual* 13: 171–183.

George, T. W. 1977. "Teacher- versus Student-Choice of Learning Activities." *Educational Research Quarterly* 2: 22–29.

Glessner, M. M. 1997. "Children's Choice in an Elementary Classroom: Ownership in the Making." Doctoral dissertation. *Dissertation Abstracts International* 58: 3423. University of North Dakota.

Howard, R. K. and M. R. Howard. 1997. "What a Difference a Choice Makes!" *Strategies* 10: 16–20.

Iyengar, S. S. and M. R. Lepper. 1999. "Rethinking the Value of Choice: A Cultural Perspective on Intrinsic Motivation." *Journal of Personality and Social Psychology* 76: 349–366.

Jervis, K. 1986. "A Teacher's Quest for a Child's Questions." *Harvard Educational Review* 56(2): 132–150.

Jolivette, K., J. H. Wehby et al. 2001. "Effects of Choice-Making Opportunities on the Behavior of Students with Emotional and Behavioral Disorders." *Behavioral Disorders* 26(2): 131–145.

Linn, M. C., B. Chen et al. 1977. "Teaching Children to Control Variables: Investigation of a Free-Choice Environment." *Journal of Research in Science Teaching* 14: 249–255.

McPhail, J. C., J. M. Pierson et al. 2000. "The Role of Interest in Fostering Sixth Grade Students' Identities as Competent Learners." *Curriculum Inquiry* 30(1): 43–70.

Appendix E

Moes, D. 1998. "Integrating Choice-Making Opportunities within Teacher-Assigned Academic Tasks to Facilitate the Performance of Children with Autism." *Journal of the Association for Persons with Severe Handicaps* 23: 319–328.

Peterson, S. M. P., C. Caniglia et al. 2001. "Application of Choice-Making Interventions for a Student with Multiply Maintained Problem Behavior." *Focus on Autism and Other Developmental Disabilities* 16: 240–246.

Powell, S. and B. Nelson. 1997. "Effects of Choosing Academic Assignments on a Student with Attention Deficit Hyperactivity Disorder." *Journal of Applied Behavior Analysis* 30: 181–183.

Rainey, R. G. 1965. "The Effects of Directed versus Non-Directed Laboratory Work on High School Chemistry Achievement." *Journal of Research in Science Teaching* 3: 286–292.

Rice, M. and M. C. Linn. 1978. "Study of Student Behavior in a Free Choice Environment." *Science Education* 62: 365–376.

Stanne, K. V. 1999. "The Effect of a Varied and Choice Curriculum on the Participation, Perceptions and Attitudes of Females in Physical Education." Doctoral dissertation. *Dissertation Abstracts International* 60: 4365. University of South Carolina.

Turner, J. C. 1995. "The Influence of Classroom Contexts on Young Children's Motivation for Literacy." *Reading Research Quarterly* 30: 410–441.

Umbreit, J. and B. Kwang-Sun. 1996. "The Effects of Preference, Choice, and Attention on Problem Behavior at School." *Education and Training in Mental Retardation and Developmental Disabilities* 31: 151–161.

Vaughn, B. J. and R. H. Horner. 1997. "Identifying Instructional Tasks that Occasion Problem Behaviors and Assessing the Effects of Student versus Teacher Choice among These Tasks." *Journal of Applied Behavior Analysis* 30: 299–312.

Whalen, S. P. and M. Csikszentmihalyi. 1991. "Putting Flow Theory into Educational Practice: The Key School's Flow Activities Room." Report to the Benton Center for Curriculum and Instruction. University of Chicago. (ERIC Document Reproduction Service no. ED338381).

Research on Providing Choice in Academic Settings

ABOUT THE AUTHOR

 Paula Denton has been an elementary school teacher since 1985 and a *Responsive Classroom* workshop presenter and consultant since 1990. She is currently on staff at Northeast Foundation for Children as a senior program developer. She has taught courses for pre-service teachers at Antioch New England Graduate School and the University of Massachusetts. She completed requirements for her EdD degree from the University of Massachusetts in spring 2005.

ABOUT THE
RESPONSIVE CLASSROOM® APPROACH

This book grew out of the work of Northeast Foundation for Children, Inc. (NEFC) and an approach to teaching known as the *Responsive Classroom* approach. Developed by classroom teachers, this approach consists of highly practical strategies for integrating social and academic learning throughout the school day.

Seven beliefs underlie this approach:

1. The social curriculum is as important as the academic curriculum.

2. How children learn is as important as what they learn: Process and content go hand in hand.

3. The greatest cognitive growth occurs through social interaction.

4. There is a specific set of social skills that children need to learn and practice in order to be successful academically and socially: cooperation, assertion, responsibility, empathy, and self-control.

5. Knowing the children we teach—individually, culturally, and developmentally—is as important as knowing the content we teach.

6. Knowing the families of the children we teach and encouraging their participation is as important as knowing the children we teach.

7. How we, the adults at school, work together to accomplish our shared mission is as important as our individual competence: Lasting change begins with the adult community.

More information and guidance on the *Responsive Classroom* approach are available through:

Publications and Resources

- Books, videos, and audios for K-8 educators
- Website with articles and other information: www.responsiveclassroom.org
- Free quarterly newsletter for educators

Professional Development Opportunities

- One-day and week-long workshops for teachers
- Classroom consultations and other services at individual schools and school districts
- Multi-faceted professional development for administrators and all staff at schools wishing to implement the *Responsive Classroom* approach school-wide

For details, contact:

RESPONSIVE CLASSROOM
NORTHEAST FOUNDATION FOR CHILDREN, INC.
85 Avenue A, Suite 204   P. O. Box 718
Turners Falls, MA 01376-0718
Phone 800-360-6332 or 413-863-8288
Fax 877-206-3952
www.responsiveclassroom.org

Rules in School

By Kathryn Brady, Mary Beth Forton, Deborah Porter, and Chip Wood

For K–8 teachers (2003) 272 pages ISBN 978-1-892989-10-9

Establish a calm, safe learning environment and teach children self-discipline with this approach to classroom rules.

- *Guidelines for creating rules with students based on their hopes and dreams for school*
- *Steps in modeling and role playing the rules* ■ *How to reinforce the rules through language*
- *Using logical consequences when rules are broken* ■ *Suggestions for teaching children to live by the rules outside the classroom*

Learning Through Academic Choice

By Paula Denton, EdD

For K–6 teachers (2005) 224 pages ISBN 978-1-892989-14-7

Enhance students' learning with this powerful tool for structuring lessons and activities.

- *Information on building a strong foundation for Academic Choice* ■ *Step-by-step look at Academic Choice in action* ■ *Practical advice for creating an Academic Choice lesson plan*
- *Many ideas for Academic Choice activities*

Parents and Teachers Working Together

By Carol Davis and Alice Yang

For K–6 teachers (2005) 232 pages ISBN 978-1-892989-15-4

Build school–home cooperation and involve parents in ways that support their children's learning.

- *Working with diverse family cultures* ■ *Building positive relationships in the early weeks of school* ■ *Keeping in touch all year long* ■ *Involving parents in classroom life, including parents who can't physically come to school* ■ *Problem-solving with parents*